MAYO CLINIC PRESS KIDS | An imprint of Mayo Clinic Press
200 First St. SW
Rochester, MN 55905
mcpress.mayoclinic.org
To stay informed about Mayo Clinic Press, please subscribe to our
free e-newsletter at MCPress.MayoClinic.org/parenting or follow us
on social media.

For bulk sales to, contact Mayo Clinic at SpecialSalesMayoBooks@mayo.edu.

**Proceeds from the sale of every book benefit important medical research
and education at Mayo Clinic.**

ISBN: 979-8-88770-044-1 (paperback) | 979-8-88770-009-0 (library
binding) | 979-8-88770-010-6 (ebook) | 979-8-88770-088-5 (multiuser PDF)
| 979-8-88770-087-8 (multiuser ePub)

Library of Congress Control Number: 2023934034

PERIOD.

The Quick Guide to *Every* Uterus

AITANA GIRÁLDEZ

RUTH REDFORD

CONTENTS

You want to put together a period pack?
Turn to page 12

You've just started your period?
Turn to page 16

curious about products you can use?
Turn to page 20

Want to know about playing sports on your period?
Turn to page 32

Worried that you haven't had your period yet?
Turn to page 36

You need help handling period pain?
Turn to page 40

INTRODUCTION

This book is easy to use.

In fact, if you turn back to the contents page you could probably skip this and find what you need to know!

But otherwise grab a seat and let's have a chat.

We cover everything about periods!

Everything?

Well, I think so. And there's some great tips for where to go if you want to learn even MORE about your period!

Periods are sometimes seen as a difficult topic to talk about, but we really want this book to make it easy-peasy.

You could look through it with a friend!

Or a grown-up.

Or just read it by yourself.

It's really up to you!

Hopefully this book will be your one-stop shop for understanding periods.

It's got information on products ...

Menstrual cups, period underwear, pads, tampons – we talk about them all!

Menstrual cups – what on earth are they?

Anyway... that is all dealt with in the relevant chapter.

It's a small silicon cup that you can insert to catch blood. It doesn't take long to get used to using them and they are surprisingly mess free!

Oh, sorry! Just trying to be helpful.

So, there is information on dealing with your very first period

There's help with any problems you might experience.

We tackle what to do when you might find a situation tricky if you're on your period...

Just remember half of the grown-up population have periods or have gone through periods.

There is nothing that you will experience that hasn't been experienced by someone else, too!

So make sure you talk to people you trust.

And never forget that your period is just your amazing body at work!

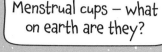

7

CHAPTER ONE
YOUR PERIOD BASICS

It's yours

Own it

LET'S TAKE A LITTLE TRIP INTO YOUR BODY...

Your reproductive system has **five** main parts.

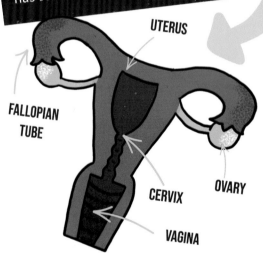

UTERUS

FALLOPIAN TUBE

CERVIX

OVARY

VAGINA

WHAT IS A PERIOD, YOU ASK?

Did I?

The **uterus** sheds its lining once a month, and the blood and mucus that comes out of your vagina is that lining.

WHO GETS A PERIOD?

I think we know the answer to this.

Well it's worth checking!

If you have a **uterus**, you will probably get your period.

WHEN IS IT GOING TO HAPPEN?

The average age is between 12 and 13 years old but you can be as young as 8 or as old as 16, and some people can start even earlier or later.

There are normally signs it will be coming soon, see page 10 for more info.

Or has it already?

I was 12 when I started.

I was 9!

I was 14. I thought it would never come.

HOW LONG DOES DOES IT LAST?

Your period will last between three to seven days and come once a month, between 28-32 days apart. This can vary and what's normal for you may be different for someone else.

It feels like forever.

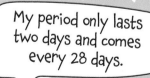

My period only lasts two days and comes every 28 days.

Don't be so melodramatic!

Mine is seven days long but comes only every 32 days.

WHAT IS PUBERTY?

Puberty means pubes!

And maturity, but that hasn't happened to you yet, has it?

You grow taller.

You start to have sexual thoughts and feelings.

Hormones might make you feel more irritable and moodier.

Your breasts and hips get bigger!

You get zits and sweat more.

Pubic hair starts to grow.

You grow armpit hair.

Your vagina will produce a clear discharge.

The hair on your legs gets darker.

You start your periods.

When does it happen and for how long?

That's a whole lot of stuff!

Usually between the ages of 8 and 14. It can take a couple of years.

Of course, you would know!

So what actually happens?

Your body starts an amazing combination of hormone shifts and physical growth. Every month your uterus starts growing a new lining of blood and other fluids.

This is to help a baby grow, and, in the absence of pregnancy, your body wants to get rid of that lining...ta da! Your period.

This is called your monthly hormone or menstrual cycle.

There are two phases. First, hormones from the brain and the ovaries ripen the egg.

Second, the egg is released (ovulation). About two weeks later, the lining of the uterus sheds and you get your period.

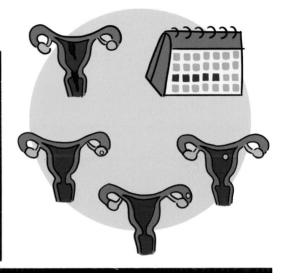

HOW HORMONES AFFECT US

ESTROGEN

The hormone estrogen increases when the egg is ripening and changes the texture of the mucus made by your cervix by making it thinner, runnier, and clearer.

When the egg isn't fertilized it just dissolves inside the Fallopian tube.

Eggs are about the same size as the period at the end of this sentence.

PROGESTERONE

When the estrogen drops another hormone called progesterone increases. This hormone makes the mucus from the cervix thick and sticky.

These hormones going up and down can affect some people's moods.

You might feel irritable, depressed, or anxious before you menstruate or have trouble controlling your emotions.

CHAPTER TWO
BEING PREPARED

So let's get ready!

Let's go!

Preparation is everything!

Here are a few things you can do to prepare for the big day.

Ewww!

The big day? It sounds like they're getting married!

Aw! Cute.

You can try on various period products, like pads or period underwear.

How does it feel?

So weird!

You can make a period pack that you have ready in your bag, just in case. (There's more information on the next page.)

It feels fine to me!

I got TONS of dark-colored underwear.

Well, leave some for me!

That's a great idea, since leaks will happen from time to time.

It's important to talk about your period.

Do we have to?

Maybe you'll learn something new!

It doesn't have to be with a parent or a grown-up. It could be a friend or an older sibling or someone you know and trust.

The main thing is to try not to feel embarrassed. It's your body. It's your period. There is nothing to be ashamed of. But if you do feel awkward, that's ok, too!

I'm really dreading getting my period.

Me too.

I can't wait!

Meh.

It's really normal to dread getting your period.

And to be looking forward to it.

How about reading a book to prepare?

Duh! That's what they're doing!

Well, it doesn't have to be just one, there are lots out there you know!

See page 44 for some recommendations.

THE PERIOD PACK!

WHAT CAN GO IN A PERIOD PACK?

Chocolate!

Maybe the least helpful thing you've said so far.

I think chocolate is a great idea.

Pads!

Tampons!

Spare underwear!

Pain relief!

Wipes!

AND WHAT IS THE PACK?

A small purse?

A pencil case?

A wallet?

A makeup bag?

Any of those things would be perfect. You just need it to be something you don't mind pulling out of your bag.

What about at home?

At home, you can organize the bathroom with everything you need. Or keep a period pack for home in your room. It's up to you!

15

CHAPTER THREE
YOUR FIRST PERIOD

How exciting!

It's the big day!

I told you not to say that!

Did you find some blood on your underwear or in the toilet?

It doesn't really look like blood, it's more brown, watery.

Mine is lots of blood.

HOW ARE YOU FEELING?

Blerg... I feel so weird!

I think everyone can tell something changed.

I want to shout it from the rooftops!

If you get your period and you have nothing with you, don't panic!

It's fine to put some toilet paper in your underwear until you get to your period pack or somewhere you can get products.

Don't forget to check the bathroom! Sometimes they have pads or tampons.

You can also ask someone. Lots of people go through this, they won't mind.

The main thing to remember is that no-one will know just by looking at you. It's not written on your face.

But you might want to tell people.

Or not...

Some people throw a period party!

That sounds so great, count me in.

Count me out, that sounds gross.

It is a good idea to tell someone you've got your period.

Sharing your problems really helps.

Are you saying it's a problem?

Oops! No... wrong saying, I guess.

?

SO WHAT NOW?

If you're finding it hard to talk about, you could just try writing it down in a note.

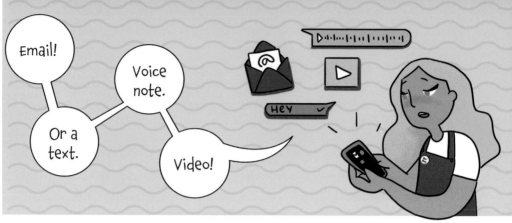

But you might need to tell a different adult, too. You need someone who has your back and you can ask them questions.

Other family members or a trusted adult.

Even a nurse or a doctor.

Or someone at school, like the school nurse!

So, are you wondering what's next?

I like to have a nice bath.

What do you mean?

Can you do that?

Won't you bleed all over the bathtub?

No! It's fine.

You might need to wash more often than usual during your period. And wash your clothes, if they get any blood on them.

Are you thinking "when will it come again?"

Well, yes!

In a month! 28 days to be exact. But not always.

And sometimes it takes a while to settle into a cycle or rhythm.

Mine came for the first time and then didn't come again until four months later.

Did you scare it off?

It's regular now, so no!

CHAPTER FOUR

MANAGING YOUR PERIOD

Let's have a product overview!

Product?

The stuff you use for your period!

PADS

You can buy stuff from supermarkets, pharmacies, or online.

Disposable pads are the first things most people use for their period.

What does disposable mean?

You throw them away.

That's right, you use them and then straight into the garbage can.

Pads have a sticky strip which sticks it to your underwear. Just don't forget to peel off the wrapping!

It won't move around?

That's right!

I've seen pads that are smaller sizes and better for younger people.

There are so many options!

Some pads are thicker so it can absorb more blood. If you just have some spotting, you could use a liner. It's much thinner but will give you peace of mind.

What if my pad leaks?

It probably will at some point during a period. It's normal!

But generally they're all the same. So, it doesn't matter what brand you use.

Some pads have these sticky wings, which wrap around underneath your underwear. This can stop some of the smaller leaks.

When I see blood on it.

If you change it every time you see blood, you'll use up pads real fast!

If it's a lot then change it.

I change mine every three hours, then I know it's not going to smell and I've got it under control.

Once you've used one and need to change it, you can wrap it up in toilet paper and pop it in the trash.

DO NOT flush it down the toilet!

If there isn't a waste basket, then just tuck it into a bag or pocket to dispose of as soon as you can.

Disposable pads are great, but you can also get reusable pads.

But how does that even work?

You wash them, silly!

In the toilet?

No! In the washing machine. You can soak them before if you like

If you use them, you'll need to work out a method for how you wash them. Start by asking a grown-up to help you.

ON TO TAMPONS!

No way!

It's a small cotton wad with a string attached that you put up into your vagina to soak up the blood.

I'd like to give that a try.

Tampons have different sizes depending on depending on how heavy your flow is too.

You should change them every six hours.

Some people prefer to use tampons once they're used to their period and have had it a few times.

Some tampons have plastic applicators which you extend and then can shoot the tampon inside you.

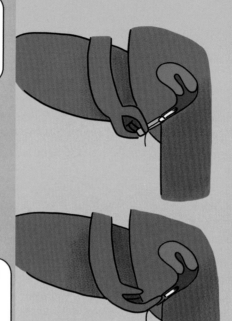

Okay, more like push the tampon in.

Some have cardboard ones!

And some have no applicator.

Those look hard!

TO PUT A TAMPON IN...

Wash your hands.

Unwrap the tampon and pull the string out straight.

Then push the tampon up inside your vagina, leaving the string dangling out.

You shouldn't be able to feel it once it's in all the way.

And don't worry, you can't push it in too far!

22

If your tampon comes with an applicator then you pull it out to extend and then put it up your vagina.

Then push the tampon up inside your vagina, leaving the string dangling out.

Once it's inside you, take the applicator out, and throw it away.

The string will be dangling out so you can pull it out when you need to change it.

When you're ready to take it out, hold the string and gently tug. Try to change your tampon every 6 hours.

Sometimes they can be hard to take out, if they haven't soaked up enough blood.

Once it's out, wrap it up in toilet paper and dispose of it in the garbage.

Sometimes the string might have gone inside you a little. That's ok, just feel where it is and then pull on it.

If you try to pull it straight down it might feel like it's stuck. If you pull towards your front, it will glide out more smoothly.

Oh! That's helpful for putting them in too!

Yes, just remember to angle toward your back when you put it in.

MENSTRUAL CUPS

The other product you can put into your vagina is a menstrual cup.

A cup?

Did they say a cup?

That's right. It's a small silicone cup with a little stem.

You fold the cup into two and use two fingers to push it up into your vagina.

Once it's inside you it opens up and forms a seal and collects any blood.

It doesn't go up as far as a tampon!

You can check that it's in place by running a finger round to check there are no squished up sides.

When you're ready to take it out, you break the seal and then pull the cup out.

Empty it, wash it out in cold water and then warm soapy water. Rinse it in cold water and then put it back up.

GREAT for the environment!

You need to sterilize the cup in boiling water or the microwave before you use it at the start of your period. But besides that, there's not much else you need to do with it and there is no garbage to dispose of.

They can be tricky to get the hang of, but it's worth trying a few different ones to see what works for you.

You can use them for up to 12 hours at a time.

I'm in!

Game changer!

I can feel it.

Hmm, it sounds like it's not in right.

The stem is poking out!

That's normal, you can trim it a little to make it shorter.

My favorite!

So easy!

Eh, they're not for me...

Period underwear have a cloth pad built into the crotch area to catch blood and discharge.

There are lots of different styles, sizes, and absorbencies.

They can take a little longer to dry.

You just wash them once you've used them and then dry them like normal underwear.

You can use with cups or tampons if your flow is very heavy.

And don't put them in the dryer!

So, logistics.

Huh?

Details!

Rinse them in cold water as soon as you're done.

CHAPTER FIVE
FAQ

Everyone will have questions!

So many...

FAQ?

Fabulous As a Queen!

No! Frequently Asked Questions.

News flash. Everyone leaks at some point.

I feel like I leak every time.

Yeah, and I have the underwear to prove it!

There are a few things you can do to try and prevent it.

Tell us!

Change your pad or product regularly?

That's one. You can also make sure you're using the right product for the amount you're bleeding in your cycle. You'll have heavier days and lighter days and you can change your product to match.

Genius!

It's hard not to feel like you smell a bit when you have your period.

But generally, nobody else can smell you.

Are you sure?

If you think the smell you have is really bad, it might be worth getting it checked out with a doctor.

It's hard not to panic if you have a stuck tampon.

Aggggghhhh!

Stop panicking!

It's going to be up there forever.

Calm down, deep breathes.

It cannot get lost, so it will come out eventually. The best thing to do is...

Wash your hands.

And try and put a finger up your vagina to find it.

Do it somewhere like the bathroom or in the shower so you be relaxed with no interruptions.

If you can't get it out, you'll need to go to a doctor or nurse.

Noooo.

It's nothing they haven't seen before.

When you get your period—or just before— your breasts can feel different.

Mine go lumpy!

No, nothing!

Mine just feel sore.

My boobs barely exist!

You're lucky, they can get in the way!

And this one is a little scary to some people: blobs of blood.

Gross!

Hey, I get blobs! I'm not gross.

I wasn't saying you were.

Oh! You mean the blobs are... well yes, they're not particularly nice!

Anyway... they're completely natural, it's just part of the uterus shedding its lining.

I was so freaked out when I saw one.

If you get tons and you're worried, you can go to the doctor and ask them to check it out, too.

So I went to the bathroom and there was all this clear mucus stuff in my underwear. What was it?

Aha! That sounds like discharge.

Discharge.

Something your body is getting rid of?

It's normal!

But I don't have my period yet and I have discharge.

Well, it's part of puberty. Your body starts to make more mucus and your vagina becomes moister.

So, what should I do?

Is it clear and white and there's not a ton of it?

Yes.

There's no bad odor or itching?

No.

Nothing! You can use a liner if it's bothering you.

If there's suddenly a lot more than usual, and you're feeling itchy or smelly down there, it's time to ask an adult or see a doctor.

Do you poo?

What's that got to do with my period?

And some of us have different poos.

This is seriously gross again.

We need to talk about it!

Noooo.

Some of us poo more when we have our period.

Ok, well here are a few hard facts! During the first couple of days of your period your body releases a hormone called prostaglandin. This helps your uterus contract and squeeze out the period blood and can also work on your intestines, making you poo more.

And so do you poo?

Yes!

It's handy to keep track of your period.

On my phone?

If you like, or go old-fashioned and do it on paper.

There are apps you can use but you need to be careful about using them because of your safety and privacy.

Even if it's irregular, it's helpful to note down when it comes and goes. Then if you ever need to talk to someone about it, you have data for them.

CHAPTER SIX
PERIOD CHALLENGES

The gameshow where you get to play...

Eeek. My period arrived and I'm at school.

Oh no, I've got tennis this afternoon and my period has just came.

Noooo, I'm staying overnight and now I've got to figure out THIS?

Ooh, that sounds fun. Can I play?

So, you're at school and suddenly you realize you've got your period.

But you've got your period pack so it's all good, yes?

And you've planned for this, so you know where all the bathrooms are.

Nope, nope and NOPE!

Well, stay calm.

Breathe!

If you don't have any products on you there's a good chance there are some available in a bathroom.

Worst case scenario grab some toilet paper and make a kind-of pad and then find someone who can help you get products as soon as possible.

You will be fine!

Just go and talk privately to the teacher.

Yeah, because it's always that easy.

If you find it too difficult to talk to the teacher, you can just ask to go to the bathroom.

Be firm; they don't want you bleeding all over the place!

And finally... make sure you go at break and lunchtime so you don't have to ask during class as often!

Check in on yourself!

I'm fine thanks.

Oh! Yes, that makes sense.

I think they mean on your pad or tampon.

Check in at break, at lunch, before after school activities, and before a long car ride.

Make sure there is a teacher or grown-up you can tell if you need to.

It's good to have someone on your side.

Tell a friend if you'd prefer, but they probably won't have as much experience dealing with everything.

If it's somewhere you stay regularly – like a parent's house – it's worth making sure you have a period pack there.

A sleepover with friends is fun.

But now I have my period.

There's no way I can go.

What if you're just honest and tell them?

Or you can just manage it and if they notice tell them.

It's not a big deal, unless you make it one!

Or they do.

That's true!

Now you're at someone's house and you have your period.

Check out if the bathroom has a trash can. If it does you can dispose of your products in the usual way, wrapped up in tissue or in a little bag.

Otherwise take it with you wrapped up and then find a trash can as soon as you can.

At night-time, try to leave some products in the bathroom so you can find them easily.

If you need some products, the best thing to do is to ask, you can do it discreetly.

Disaster, you bled through onto someone else's sheets!

I just want to run away.

They'll be so mad.

But it's actually ok. You just need to deal with it and say that you're sorry it happened and can you help wash them.

They really shouldn't be mad. It's probably happened to them before.

Try not to let it bother you. It happens to millions of people.

You'll survive!

Just don't go to sleep?

Very clever, but not practical!

Use thicker pads?

Yes, you can use thicker pads and period underwear as a double protector.

Dark pjs would be handy.

That's a plan!

THINGS YOU MIGHT NEED TO DO TO MAKE YOUR LIFE EASIER!

Empty the bathroom trash when you're on your period.

Change sheets and help with laundry more.

Keep stocked up with products. If you live between two houses, make sure both parents or caregivers know that you need monthly supplies.

Stay on top of your underwear. If you're running low, make sure you get them cleaned. If you need more, then ask to buy some.

CHAPTER SEVEN
COMMON WORRIES

Getting your period isn't always straightforward

So let's talk about some common worries you might have.

I haven't even got my period yet.

Mine are all over the place, they're so irregular.

I haven't had one in a while... am I pregnant?

Can I stop my periods?

Mine are so heavy, it's really hard work.

One at a time! Let's work this out.

You haven't got your period yet.

That's me!

And me. All my friends got theirs.

Well, if you're worried there are a few things you can do.

Check in with yourself.

If you've grown taller, developed breasts and pubic hair, then you're going through puberty — just maybe a little slower than you'd like.

There are medical and physical conditions that might delay or result in no periods.

Excessive exercise!

Insufficient nutrition.

Huh?

When you're really underweight and don't get enough food.

But, in some cases, it is worth seeing a medical professional to see if they can figure out what's going on.

Did you start puberty by the time you were 10, but you're now 14 and nothing has happened — period-wise?

Or did you start puberty by the time you were 14 but you're now 16 and nothing?

They might run some hormone tests for you.

I can't go to the doctor, it's so embarrassing.

It will be fine. They'll just ask you some questions.

Like about if you've started puberty. And things about your general health.

You can take a trusted grown-up with you, too.

Your periods are irregular.

This is really normal, especially when you first start. They can take up to two years to find a rhythm. Even if they seemed regular at first

It feels like a dream that I got my period at all! Will it ever be back?

Of course it will.

The menstrual cycle is counted in days, from the first day of one period to the first day of your next period.

It's not the same each time. It can vary from between 22 and 45 days when you're a teenager. And 22 and 35 days once your body has stopped growing.

Something that can cause your periods to become irregular is stress.

That's not me. I'm so chill.

It's me... I just feel stressed all the time.

If your cycle becomes irregular, or has never been regular, and in the two years since your first period, then it's worth speaking to a medical professional.

And they will find it very helpful if you have some data to share.

Dates of when you had a period and how long for, that sort of thing.

Are you pregnant?

I've never had sex!

Well, that will be a 'no' then!

But why have my periods stopped?

Stress!

Big life changes.

Not eating enough.

If your cycle becomes irregular, or has never been regular, and in the two years since your first period, then it's worth speaking to a medical professional. They can set your mind at rest.

NOW, WHO WANTED TO STOP THEIR PERIOD?

Me!

It's holding me back.

Doesn't everyone?

It's hard to do what I want to when I'm on my period.

It is possible to stop your periods.

You might have a medical reason.

Or you might just need a break from them.

Sometimes periods can cause distress because of gender identity.

If this is you it's best to talk to a trusted grown-up or a doctor so they can help you figure out what will work for you.

Ooh but it's not safe to stop them.

It actually is safe not to have a monthly period, but that's something to discuss with a trusted medical professional.

Who has periods that are **really heavy**?

I don't just have blood but these blobs that come out too. It's a bit scary.

That can be normal.

But it's so heavy I don't think I can leave the house.

You should check it out with a doctor.

If your periods last for longer than eight days every month and you have to change pads or tampons every hour – or if you have blobs that are larger than a quarter? Then you definitely should talk to a medical professional.

It's hard to do what I want to when I'm on my period.

It's hard but sometimes people do have heavy periods.

Like me.

And me!

CHAPTER EIGHT
PMS

So these are all classic symptoms of PMS (Premenstrual Syndrome).

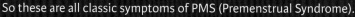

You can also just make time to have some space and snuggle up.
Relax and chill. If you need some mild painkillers, take them, too.

I just feel a bit achy and sore.

I've got awful cramps.

That's your uterus contracting and getting the lining out effectively.

Well, it's feeling a bit too effective!

Is that why I'm pooping more too?

It's all happening, and I want to crawl back into bed!

Look after yourself. Most people don't have more than a couple of days of period pain.

Take mild painkillers if you need them.

I like to use a hot water bottle and hold it on my tummy.

I like to get into a warm bath.

Favorite movie, chocolate, and snuggles!

I find exercising helps.

What?!

No, I do, too!

It makes me think about something else, which helps!

Doing some mindful breathing techniques really works for me.

41

IRREGULAR PERIOD, ACNE, AND BODY HAIR

Well, what is it then?

You need to talk to a doctor.

PCOS or Polycystic Ovary Syndrome affects a lot of people throughout their lives.

Ok, so I'll check that out on the internet.

Unless it's a trustworthy source?

So what is it?

Not so fast! PCOS is very different for kids and adults, so the internet isn't a good substitute for a doctor and a diagnosis.

Exactly.

PCOS is a condition when your hormones are unbalanced. This can lead to various symptoms.

Such as?

Irregular periods.

Excessive body or facial hair – this is caused by too much of the hormone testosterone.

Bad acne!

PCOS is diagnosed by having irregular periods more than 35 days apart or less than 21 days. But this is mostly if it's been about 3 years since your first period.

Not on a teenager! Your body is still growing and developing. That would only be used to diagnose an adult.

I heard they can do a scan to check if you have cysts on your ovaries.

So what can you do about PCOS?

Treatment is normally to go on the pill because this can help the hormone imbalance.

Exercise and weight management can help, too.

PCOS is one of the most common causes of female infertility.

Many people don't know they have it until they start trying to have a baby.

However, PCOS only affects a small amount of teenagers.

What about TSS?

Toxic shock syndrome? It's extremely rare, but worth knowing about.

It's a bacterial infection.

It happens when tampons are left inside too long, causing bacteria to multiply and release a toxin.

Symptoms are a high fever, vomiting, diarrhea, rash, muscle aches, and headaches.

It can be serious so you need to get checked out quickly if you think you have TSS.

But it is rare.

To prevent it, make sure you change your tampon every six hours and wash your hands before and after changing.

And it's worth knowing about endometriosis.

That's when the lining in your uterus grows outside of it?

Sort of. Tissue that is similar to the lining of your uterus grows outside in other parts of the body, like your ovaries and fallopian tubes.

The main symptom is period-like pain.

It can last for days.

It doesn't go away when I take painkillers.

The main thing to do if you suspect you have endometriosis is to get checked out by a medical professional.

OK.

HERE ARE SOME HELPFUL TIPS FOR YOU

Yay— here we come.

On it! Thanks!

Go it!

You can follow these tags online for empowering and helpful tips.

#freetheperiod
#menstrualmovement
#periodpower
#endperiodpoverty
#menstruationmatters

#periodpositive
#periodpowerful
#menstrualequity
#bloodygoodperiod

These might also be helpful.

AMAZE.ORG
PERIOD.ORG

You may want to find ways to limit the impact of period products on the environment.

Or just make sure you try and dispose of everything properly – never flush sanitary products down the toilet.

And give yourself a break! You've only just started having to deal with this. Once you've got your period figured out, you can think about making it more environmentally friendly.

You can make sure you recycle all the packing that you can, as most tampons come in cardboard boxes.

Use tampons with cardboard applicators instead of than plastic.

Try to find organic, pure cotton tampons – but know they're more expensive.

Look for pads with less packaging that don't use bleaching

GLOSSARY

Applicator
This comes with tampons and is a plastic or cardboard tube to help insert the tampon.

Bloating
The feeling of fullness or swelling in the belly caused by water retention, which can make the stomach look or feel bigger than usual.

Blood Clot
We've used the word blobs but clots is a good description of a clump of blood that has become a bit solid, a little like jelly.

Cervix
It's a narrow part of the uterus, at the bottom.

Contraceptive
There are many forms of these and they are designed to stop pregnancy. Condoms, IUD, and the pill are a few examples. The pill can also be prescribed to help with hormonal imbalances or for other reasons.

Cramp
You can experience these all over your body but with reference to your period it's normally in your stomach when your muscles spasm.

Cycle
This is not about a bike! Your menstrual cycle is a circular event, and you will always be at some point of it.

Disharge
Once you start puberty, discharge will come out of your vagina. It's normally pale to clear colored fluid.

Egg
Produced by the ovaries this is the female reproductive cell which needs to be fertilized with sperm (the male reproductive cell) for pregnancy.

Endometriosis
A condition where tissue similar to the uterus lining grows outside of the uterus.

Heavy
This can be about your period flow, the opposite of light!

Menstrual Products
This describes sanitary items used for periods such as tampons, pads, cups etc.

Menstruation
This is the medical term for period and describes the discharge of blood and other matter from the vagina.

PMS
Premenstrual syndrome is the symptoms (physical and emotional) you can experience before a period.

Polycystic Ovary Syndrome
A medical condition that can cause irregular periods.

Prostagladin
This period hormone can cause sickness, cramps, and more pooping during menstruation.

Puberty
A time in adolescence or late childhood where you body starts to make hormones, which can affect the body in various ways, including hair growth and mood changes.

Shedding
The uterus lining comes away as a period, this is also known as shedding.

Spotting
Sometimes small spots of blood can appear outside of your period.

TIPS FOR ADULTS

Talking to a child about periods can be daunting.

They can:

- Get very embarrassed.
- Want to know everything and ask awkward questions.
- Pretend you're not there.

Well, it's tough being a kid!

It's good to start a conversation.

It doesn't have to cover everything right away.

Just let them know you're willing to talk.

Buying some period products and making sure it's clear where they are kept is helpful.

Just a few pads would do at first.

Put them in the bathroom but maybe not on display if it feels awkward.

If you feel something might be wrong it's best to try and work out together if medical help is needed.

Having a medical professional listen and diagnose can be the most reassuring thing.

Encouraging good hygiene and washing of clothes/sheets, etc. can be helpful.

You can show them how to use the laundry – win for you!

Sharing your experience is helpful but it might not be needed right away.

What is helpful is knowing that it's different for many people.

And that you're there for them.

Basher History™

NATIONAL PARKS

KINGFISHER
LONDON & NEW YORK

KINGFISHER
LONDON & NEW YORK

Text and design copyright © Toucan Books Ltd. 2022
Based on an original concept by Toucan Books Ltd.
Illustrations copyright © Simon Basher 2022

Published in the United States by Kingfisher,
120 Broadway, New York, NY 10271
Kingfisher is an imprint of Macmillan Children's Books, London.
All rights reserved.

EU representative: 1st Floor, The Liffey Trust Centre,
117-126 Sheriff Street Upper, Dublin 1 D01 YC43

Designed and created by Basher www.basherscience.com
Text written by Joe Yogerst

Dedication: Voor onze lieve buren uit de Kerkstraat

Distributed in the U.S. and Canada by Macmillan,
120 Broadway, New York, NY 10271

Library of Congress Cataloging-in-Publication data has been applied for.

ISBN: 978-0-7534-7843-1

Kingfisher books are available for special promotions and premiums.
For details contact: Special Markets Department, Macmillan,
120 Broadway, New York, NY 10271.

For more information, please visit www.kingfisherbooks.com

Printed in China
10 9 8 7 6 5 4 3 2 1
1TR/0122/WKT/RV/128MA

CONTENTS

Introduction
The birth of the national park

The Scottish-American naturalist John Muir once wrote, "Everyone needs beauty as well as bread, places to play in and pray in where nature may heal and cheer and give strength to body and soul alike." He was talking about his beloved Yosemite Valley, and he was thinking that many more places needed to be preserved as spots where people could discover the wilderness and reconnect with nature.

In 1903, Muir invited President Theodore Roosevelt to visit Yosemite to discuss his idea. Camped beneath the Mariposa Grove redwood trees near Glacier Point, talking around the campfire at night, the two great men decided that America needed a system of national parks stretching from Atlantic to Pacific. Roosevelt declared some using his presidential power—Crater Lake in Oregon and Mesa Verde in Colorado. But it wasn't until 1916 that Congress created the National Park System. At first, natural landmarks like Zion, Grand Canyon, and Hawaii Volcanoes became national parks, but the idea eventually extended to historical and cultural landmarks, too. Today, true to John Muir's original vision, there are 63 American national parks, and the U.S. National Park System manages more than 420 sites, ranging from seashores and battlefields to wild and scenic rivers and recreation areas.

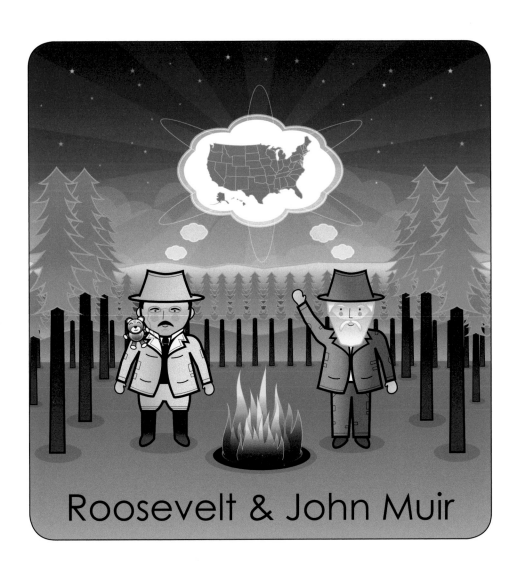

Roosevelt & John Muir

Chapter 1
The Northeast

This region is BIG on American history. Many of its parks are about people and events. At Minute Man National Historical Park, you can stand where the American Revolution began. Gettysburg National Military Park is the site of a major turning point in the Civil War and Abraham Lincoln's most famous speech. The Statue of Liberty & Ellis Island welcomed millions of immigrants to America, while Thomas Edison invented recorded music and movies in his New Jersey lab. Oh, and there are natural wonders, too! From Acadia in Maine to New River Gorge in West Virginia, you're going to see some real beauties!

Cape Cod

Acadia

New River Gorge

Statue of Liberty & Ellis Island

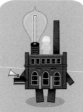

Thomas Edison

Saint-Gaudens

National Mall

Assateague Island

Gettysburg

Minute Man

Cape Cod
National Seashore, Massachusetts

- ☀ Elbow-shaped peninsula known for its shipwrecks
- ☀ Has wetlands, forests, and 40 miles (64 km) of beach
- ☀ Great white sharks feed in its waters in summer

Plymouth Rock tries to take the credit, but *I'm* the first place the Pilgrims landed in the New World. They spent five weeks scoping things out before sailing west across Plymouth Bay. Those *Mayflower* folk didn't really appreciate me. There wasn't enough fresh water, they nearly clashed with my Native American friends, and they found my ocean waters too rough. They were right about the last one—since they left, I've seen more than 1000 shipwrecks.

It took a couple of hundred years, but humans do dig my sandy shore. Some built sturdy lighthouses to keep ships from crashing into me, while others established a famous artist colony in my dunes. And Guglielmo Marconi, the fellow who invented wireless communication, used me for the first two-way radio message across an ocean in 1903.

- ● The *Mayflower* and its Pilgrims dropped anchor on November 11, 1620
- ● Today, millions of people visit Cape Cod for surf, sun, and sand vacations
- ● Marconi connected President Teddy Roosevelt to King Edward VII of the U.K.

Cape Cod

Acadia
■ National Park, Maine

☀ First national park east of the Mississippi River
☀ Occupies two islands and the mainland Schoodic Peninsula
☀ With 338 bird species, it's a prime spot for bird-watchers

Home sweet home! I'm on the second-largest island along the East Coast. French explorers named it Isle des Monts Deserts, or Island of Desert Mountains, for its treeless peaks. One of those summits—Cadillac Mountain—is the place to catch the earliest sunrise in the U.S. in winter.

Sunrise-seeking humans aren't my only early birds. My strategic coastal location between the New England mainland and the open ocean, and along the Atlantic Flyway between the Arctic and the Caribbean, means I get visited by millions of birds from different regions. With an eagle eye, you might spy winged wonders such as the snowy owl, dark-eyed junco, yellow-bellied sapsucker, and the common loon with its haunting cry. Every spring, I close a number of hiking trails to protect peregrine falcon nests.

● Crossed by 45 miles (72 km) of bike-and-hike-only cobblestone carriage roads
● At 1530 ft (465 m) tall, Cadillac is the highest of 26 Acadia mountains
● Tiny Baker Island harbors a lighthouse, cemetery, and pioneer homes

Acadia

New River Gorge
■ National Park & Preserve, West Virginia

✳ Longest and deepest canyon in the Appalachian Mountains
✳ Some of the wildest whitewater rafting in the eastern U.S.
✳ Spanned by a world-record steel-arch bridge

I'm the nation's newest national park, a status I achieved in 2021 after many years as a national scenic river. Whitewater fans come from far and wide to ride my turbulent waters. My upper river is mellow enough for newbies, but my lower river is a liquid beast, 16 miles (26 kilometers) of raging water through the deepest of canyons. My rapids—some of them long, difficult, and violent—have funny names like Screaming Eddy and Big Baloney.

You know the roller-coaster river ride is over when you see the New River Gorge Bridge looming high above. It's one of the world's five longest single-span steel-arch bridges. Even more impressive is the fact that it flies 876 feet (267 meters) above the water—perfect for an even scarier adventure sport: BASE jumping off the bridge with a parachute. Yikes!

● New River is one of the world's oldest rivers (more than 300 million years old)
● BASE jumping is allowed only during the annual Bridge Day Festival in October
● Thurmond Historic District preserves the remains of a coal-mining ghost town

New River Gorge

Statue of Liberty & Ellis Island

National Monument, New York & New Jersey

* Symbol of American freedom, equality, and democracy
* Completed in 1886 after 21 years of construction
* Stands 151 ft (46 m) tall from torch to toe

Made in France—to celebrate the 100th anniversary of the American Revolution—I have become a towering symbol of the United States and the millions of immigrants who have moved here to escape poverty, political strife, and other troubles in their homelands. I never tire of raising my giant copper torch high above New York Harbor.

That tablet in my left hand is inscribed "July 4, 1776" to mark the signing of the Declaration of Independence. Beneath my feet, a broken chain signifies the end of slavery. From this little island, I gaze at the harbor entrance that so many new Americans have sailed through. And I'm not alone. Beside me is the immigration station on Ellis Island, where around 12 million people checked into the United States.

- Official name: *La Liberté éclairant le monde* (*Liberty Enlightening the World*)
- Ellis Island welcomed immigrants from 1892 to 1954
- Lady Liberty is covered in 62,000 lb (28,000 kg) of copper

Statue of Liberty
& Ellis Island

Thomas Edison

■ National Historical Park, New Jersey

☀ Edison's factory and inventions workshop from 1887 to 1931
☀ Contains hundreds of amazing 20th-century inventions
☀ The park is also home to Edison's Glenmont residence

Beyond my redbrick walls, my labs and workshops lie almost untouched (albeit a little dustier) since the day the factory closed in 1931. Edison conceived the lightbulb before setting up here, but he had plenty of other bright ideas. Besides coffeepots, toasters, and waffle irons, he developed the world's first music phonograph, a movie studio, and a battery for electric cars.

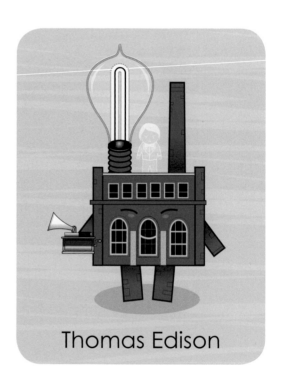

Thomas Edison

● Edison registered an incredible 1093 patents for new inventions
● He called the home appliances he developed "electric servants"
● His first film was a five-second clip of a man sneezing

Saint-Gaudens

■ National Historical Park, New Hampshire

* Celebrates legendary sculptor Augustus Saint-Gaudens
* Located in New Hampshire's scenic Connecticut River Valley
* Saint-Gaudens' home and studio from 1885 to 1907

Saint-Gaudens

I'm one of those rare parks that revolves around an artist. Augustus Saint-Gaudens created some of America's best-known sculptures, including a legendary statue of Abraham Lincoln for a Chicago park. He also designed coins for the U.S. Mint, including the famous Double Eagle gold coin of 1905–07. Come and admire his work in the Little Studio and around the grounds.

● Sculpture workshops, summer concerts, and modern art exhibitions are held here
● Saint-Gaudens inspired the nearby Cornish Colony and its hundreds of artists
● The site has two hiking trails through more than 100 acres (40 ha.) of forest

National Mall
Washington, DC

* Massive park in the middle of the nation's capital
* Shaded by 9000 trees—mostly elms and cherry trees
* Home to the Washington Monument and Lincoln Memorial

No, I am *not* a shopping mall, but a long, rectangular green space that architect Pierre L'Enfant included in his plan for Washington, DC in 1791. Back then, cows and other livestock grazed my grassy glades. Moooooo!

It wasn't until the Washington Monument was finished in 1884 that people started to take me seriously as a national treasure. Other landmarks followed, from the Lincoln Memorial and Smithsonian Institute to the Vietnam Veterans Memorial and National Museum of African American History & Culture. I've witnessed my fair share of American history: British Redcoats burning the White House during the War of 1812, Dr. Martin Luther King, Jr.'s "I Have a Dream Speech," a good number of presidential inaugurations, and even a Britney Spears concert.

* The mall is flanked by the White House, U.S. Capitol Building, and 14 museums
* It also features softball and rugby fields, and beach volleyball courts
* Some 3800 festivals, protests, and other events are held on the Mall each year

National Mall

Assateague Island

■ National Seashore, Maryland & Virginia

- ☀ Barrier island with pristine beaches and wild horses
- ☀ Two-thirds in Maryland, one-third in Virginia
- ☀ Separated from the mainland by a hurricane in 1933

I love horsing around—on my long Atlantic beaches, in the wetlands along my western shore, and especially with the wild mustangs that gallop across my sands. I've got around 300 shaggy-tailed companions. To keep their population in check, which preserves my fragile ecosystem, "saltwater cowboys" round them up once a year during the Pony Penning Festival.

Assateague Island

- ● Some people say the horses' equine ancestors survived a shipwreck
- ● Others say English settlers let them roam free to avoid a tax on fences
- ● The Pony Penning Festival & Swim takes place every July on the Virginia side

Gettysburg
■ National Military Park, Pennsylvania

✴ Honors the Battle of Gettysburg, July 1–3, 1863
✴ The fighting involved 160,000 troops and 120 generals
✴ Considered one of the most haunted places in America

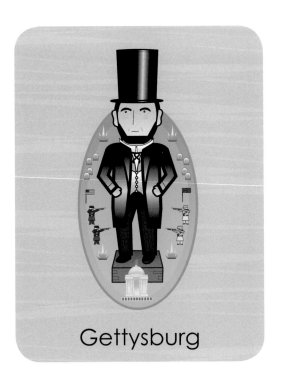

Gettysburg

Each July, I reenact the Battle of Gettysburg of 1863, a three-day clash that helped the North win the Civil War and preseve the United States as a single nation. Four months later, President Abraham Lincoln delivered his famous Gettysburg Address at the official opening of the battlefield cemetery. Today, I host monuments and museum exhibits to honor these great events.

● President Lincoln delivered his Gettysburg Address on November 19, 1863
● Lincoln's epic address was just 272 words long
● It was later discovered that female soldiers fought on both sides at Gettysburg

Minute Man
■ National Historical Park, Massachusetts

☀ Marks the spot where the American Revolution started
☀ Honors the "minutemen" who defeated the British Army
☀ Forest trails pass significant battle landmarks

I was a laidback blend of farms and forest until April 19, 1775, when rebellious Massachusetts minutemen faced off against British troops at the Old North Bridge in Concord. The Redcoats had marched up from Boston looking for weapons the American rebels had stored in their basements and barns. Nobody knows who fired the first musket, but it started the American Revolution.

Nowadays, the route is called the Battle Road, a 5-mile (8 kilometer) trail through the woods. It passes the spot where Paul Revere was captured at the end of his legendary "British are coming!" ride and the Bloody Angle where the minutemen ambushed retreating Redcoats. Then there's the Old North Bridge—as sturdy today as it was nearly 250 years ago, and the best selfie spot in the park.

● The majority of minutemen were volunteers—local farmers and shopkeepers
● *Little Women* author Louisa May Alcott grew up in the park's Wayside house
● Redcoats interrogated Revere and took his horse but let him go the same day

Minute Man

Chapter 2
The South

It seems impossible that a single region could contain national parks with snowy mountains and coral reefs, slippery salamanders and stealthy alligators. But that's the South! Located along one of the world's oldest mountain ranges—the Appalachians—Shenandoah and Great Smoky Mountains are typical forest parks with hiking and camping. Florida offers a whole different vibe: you can snorkel with tropical fish in the Dry Tortugas or encounter 'gators and manatees in the Everglades. There's history, too, with the pirate Jean Lafitte and the legendary African-American pilots, educators, and inventors of Tuskegee.

Jean Lafitte

Everglades

Cumberland Island

Great Smoky Mountains

Shenandoah

Hot Springs

Mammoth Cave

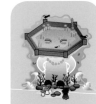

Dry Tortugas

Natchez Trace

Tuskegee Airmen & Institute

Jean Lafitte

National Historical Park & Preserve, Louisiana

* Named for a pirate who fought in the Battle of New Orleans
* Features six separate parts spread across southern Louisiana
* Celebrates traditional food, dance, music, and Cajun French

Sure, I'm named for a French pirate, but there's more to me than talking parrots and tales of buried treasure. My six sections highlight different aspects of local nature and culture. Walk the planks of the boardwalk trail at Bayou Barataria, and you'll see pristine wetlands with turtles and alligators. Or shiver your timbers while dancing to old-time Cajun music at the Prairie Acadian Cultural Center.

Weigh anchor on a Mississippi paddle-wheeler in New Orleans and cruise downriver to Chalmette Battlefield, where Lafitte helped Andrew Jackson beat the British in the 1815 Battle of New Orleans. In return, the pirates were granted pardons for their crimes and many became law-abiding citizens. But Lafitte longed for the pirate's life and returned to his swashbuckling ways. Aaaarrrrgggghhhh!

- A "Rendez-vous des Cajuns" show features live Cajun and Zydeco bands
- Cajuns trace their roots to French Acadians expelled from Canada in the 1700s
- Lafitte left Louisiana and established a new pirate base along the Texas coast

Jean Lafitte

Everglades
■ National Park, Florida

✴ This biosphere reserve features nine natural habitats
✴ Thirty-nine endangered species call the park home
✴ Includes 100s of small islands in the Gulf of Mexico

I like to think of myself as the Subtropical Trickster. I may look like a giant grassland, but I'm really a shallow, super-wide river flowing across Florida to the Gulf of Mexico. From the Seminole people to modern park rangers, humans have called me home for thousands of years.

I'm known for my wildlife. Among my beasty besties are American alligators, West Indian manatees, the very rare Florida panthers, and a swimming bunny called the marsh rabbit. Come and stay in one of my campgrounds, but if you come across a "hammock," don't climb aboard for a nap. That's because an Everglades hammock is a junglelike island of trees surrounded by wetlands. The best way to see me is paddling a canoe through my maze of waterways. With a sharp eye out for 'gators, of course!

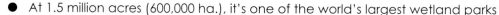

● At 1.5 million acres (600,000 ha.), it's one of the world's largest wetland parks
● Its natural habitats include mangrove swamp, pineland, and flooded forest
● The largest alligator ever found at Everglades was 17 ft, 5 in (5 m) long

Everglades

Cumberland Island

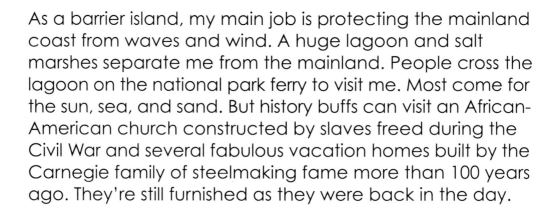

National Seashore, Georgia

* Barrier island with wetlands, forest, and miles of beach
* Inhabited by wild horses, sea turtles, and horseshoe crabs
* Once home to freed slaves and steelmaking tycoons

Wild horses couldn't drag me away from this supercool spot on the Georgia coast. Not even the ones who gallop along my pristine beach. The sand stretches for 17 miles (27 kilometers) on my Atlantic side—one of the longest undeveloped beaches along the Eastern Seaboard.

As a barrier island, my main job is protecting the mainland coast from waves and wind. A huge lagoon and salt marshes separate me from the mainland. People cross the lagoon on the national park ferry to visit me. Most come for the sun, sea, and sand. But history buffs can visit an African-American church constructed by slaves freed during the Civil War and several fabulous vacation homes built by the Carnegie family of steelmaking fame more than 100 years ago. They're still furnished as they were back in the day.

● The wild horses may be related to Spanish or English colonial ponies
● Snakes, 'gators, and more than 300 bird species inhabit the salt marshes
● The island's ghostly Dungeness mansion was destroyed by fire in 1959

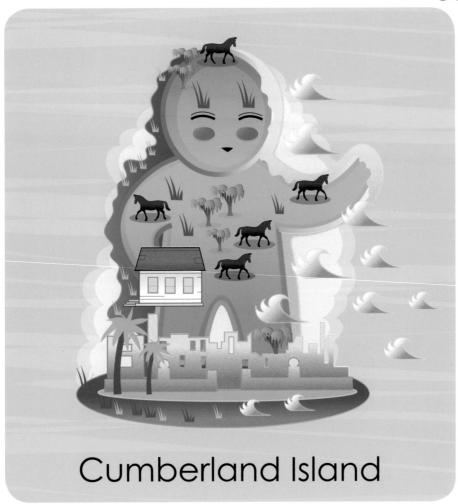

Cumberland Island

Great Smoky Mountains

National Park, North Carolina & Tennessee

- Ancient mountain wilderness with huge biodiversity
- Most visited national park, with 12.5 million visitors per year
- "Salamander Capital" of the world

That's not really smoke hovering over my ridges and valleys. It's a bluish haze caused by a combination of high humidity, frequent rain, and tiny organic chemicals released by the billions of plants that cover me. How green are my thumbs? I'm talking more than 1600 species of flowering plants, 100 different native trees, plus hundreds of nonflowering mosses and some 50 ferns.

Thousands of critters call me home. My favorites are the slippery salamanders that live along my rivers and streams. I have 30 species ranging from the little-finger-size pygmy salamander to a ginormous hellbender salamander that can weigh as much as a small dog or cat.

- Great Smoky has hosted the popular Spring Wildflower Pilgrimage since 1950
- The Appalachian Trail follows a roller-coaster route across the park's peaks
- Scientists estimate there are 80,000 to 100,000 plant and animal species here

Great Smoky Mountains

Shenandoah

■ National Park, Virginia

☀ Protects 300 square miles (800 km²) of the Blue Ridge Mountains
☀ Features a scenic meandering, mountaintop Skyline Drive
☀ Largely created during the Great Depression

Part of the Appalachian Range, my Blue Ridge Mountains are some of Earth's oldest peaks. But I wasn't established until 1935. That makes me a child of the Great Depression, a time when the world economy crashed and millions of people were out of work. Some of them signed up for a program called the Civilian Conservation Corps (CCC) that helped create national, state, and city parks.

Hundreds of CCC workers built my cabins, campgrounds, and a spectacular mountaintop road called Skyline Drive. President Herbert Hoover used to visit each summer to get away from the heat, humidity, and heavy politics in nearby Washington, DC. His "Summer White House" was a log cabin at Camp Rapidan. Tucked into a remote valley, it can be reached only by foot or horse from Skyline Drive.

● An extensive hiking network includes 100 miles (160 km) of the Appalachian Trail
● Some 300 to 500 black bears inhabit the park
● Black parkgoers had to use a segregated campsite and facilities until 1950

Shenandoah

Hot Springs
■ National Park, Arkansas

☀ Forty-seven natural springs with water averaging 143°F (62°C)
☀ Historic bathhouses with swimming pools and steamy caves
☀ First nature area protected by the federal government (1832)

For hundreds of years, people have been using my naturally warm spring water to cure ailments, soothe muscles, or simply relax. Native Americans and early settlers soaked in a natural outdoor setting of the Ouachita Mountains. The Victorians built fancy indoor pools. Two of those old-timey spas still welcome visitors to try their thermal pools, private baths, and steam cave.

Hot Springs

● Thomas Jefferson dispatched an expedition in 1804 to find the springs
● The springs gush around 700,000 gallons (2.7 million liters) of water each day
● Blue-green algae and ostracods (small crustaceans) live in the spring water

Mammoth Cave

■ National Park, Kentucky

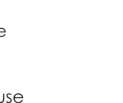

✳ World's longest-known cave system (412 miles/663 km)
✳ Began forming around 10 to 15 million years ago
✳ More than 200 other (smaller) caves surround the big one

Mammoth Cave

I'm known for my big mouth, and not because I talk a lot. I have a huge entrance that leads into an even bigger belly. The walls and the rock formations that decorate my many rooms are made of limestone dissolved by acidic water that slowly seeps from the surface. My animal friends include bats, spiders, cave shrimp, salamanders, and eyeless cave fish. Euch!

● Over 30 miles (48 km) of the Green and Nolin rivers run through the park
● Native Americans first entered the cave around 5000 years ago
● Some of the earliest Mammoth Cave guides were enslaved African Americans

Dry Tortugas
National Park, Florida

* Seven-island archipelago in the Gulf of Mexico
* Part of the world's third-longest coral reef system
* America's largest masonry (brickwork) fort

Unless you're the world's best swimmer, the only way to reach me is by boat or seaplane. That's because I'm located in the Gulf of Mexico at the western end of the Florida Keys. My half-English/half-Spanish name derives from the fact that European explorers found lots of sea turtles (*tortugas*) but no drinking water when they visited. That didn't prevent pirates or cargo ships from cruising my waters . . . or wrecking on my jagged coral reefs.

The Americans who bought Florida (and me) from Spain in 1819 spent nearly 30 years constructing Fort Jefferson on Garden Key, one of my larger islands. Like some giant LEGO set, it's made with 16 million bricks. It's so big and menacing that no one has ever tried to attack it, not even the Confederates during the Civil War.

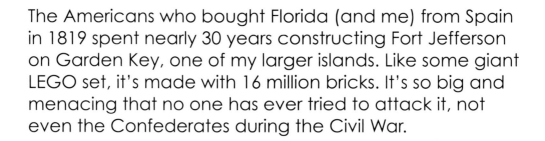

- The remains of at least 275 ships lie beneath the park's beautiful blue waters
- Around 80,000 sooty terns nest every year on the park's Bush Key island
- Staghorn, elkhorn, and fan are among the Dry Tortugas' 30 coral species

Dry Tortugas

Natchez Trace

Parkway, Mississippi, Alabama, & Tennessee

* This skinny 444-mile-long (715 km) park crosses three states
* Brimming with natural and human history
* Construction began in 1938, during the Great Depression

You can drive my entire length on a ribbon of highway between Nashville and Natchez city, but I was once just a buffalo track followed by Native Americans and then a rough dirt road that carried traders, trappers, soldiers, and settlers across a remote wilderness that had only recently become part of the U.S. Tiny stretches of that old road survive, as do Native American mounds and village sites, early American homes and pioneer farms, Civil War graves and the place where explorer Meriwether Lewis is buried.

While visitors love to hike my forest, waterfall, and swamp trails, they also travel along me on a journey through musical history. Elvis Presley was raised just a few miles off my route, Nashville is the undisputed capital of country music, and my western end is where Delta blues was born.

● The Trace may originally have been formed by bison herds seeking salt licks
● Centuries of traffic have caused parts of the Trace to sink deep into the ground
● There's not a single stop sign or traffic light along the entire Trace

Natchez Trace

Tuskegee Airmen & Institute

■ National Historical Sites, Alabama

✳ Training ground for Black American military pilots during WWII
✳ Site of a historically Black college and university (HBCU)
✳ Has museums dedicated to pioneering African Americans

I have two sites, celebrated for very different skills. The Tuskegee Airmen of WWII fame earned their wings at an airfield on the outskirts of Tuskegee town. Nicknamed the "Red Tails" because of the distinctive red markings on their airplanes, they were the first African-American military pilots. The airmen participated in more than 1500 combat missions during the war, earning numerous medals for their bravery.

Just 6 miles (10 kilometers) away, the Tuskegee Institute was founded in 1881 as a college for Black students who, at that point in American history, weren't allowed to attend many universities. Under the leadership of institute president Booker T. Washington, Tuskegee also grew into an important research institution.

● Two of the original Tuskegee airfield hangars are now museums
● Scientist George Washington Carver was a renowned Tuskegee Institute professor
● Booker T. Washington and George Washington Carver were born into slavery

Tuskegee Airmen & Institute

Chapter 3
The Midwest

The Midwest was left behind in the early-20th-century rush to create more parks. But the region is quickly making up for lost time. You'll find several of the newest parks—Indiana Dunes along the shore of Lake Michigan and Ice Age National Scenic Trail in Wisconsin, among others—located amid the Great Lakes and the Great Plains. Midwest parks also preserve two American icons: Mount Rushmore and the Gateway Arch. And if you're interested in seeing some of the nation's oldest objects, you need look no further than the ancient Native American artwork of Effigy Mounds and the prehistoric bones of Agate Fossil Beds.

Isle Royale

Agate Fossil Beds

Effigy Mounds

Voyageurs

Ice Age

Mount Rushmore

Gateway Arch

Theodore
Roosevelt

Indiana Dunes

Isle Royale
■ National Park, Michigan

❋ In Lake Superior, North America's largest freshwater lake
❋ Renowned for its resident moose and timber wolves
❋ Scuba divers like to explore its 10 famous shipwrecks

Call me a riddle. I'm undeniably American but live much closer to Canada. I belong to Michigan but could easily be Minnesotan. As one of the most remote national parks, few people live on or visit me these days. But years ago, I had a lot of roomies: Native American copper hunters, French trappers who named me for King Louis XIV, early American fishermen and miners, and lighthouse keepers who tried to prevent ships from crashing into my rocky shores.

My other mystery is how big animals such as moose, wolves, caribou, and lynx reached me. A gold-medal swimmer of the animal kingdom, moose likely swam the 15 miles (24 kilometers) from Canada during the spring or summer. The others, far less able, probably waited for winter and walked across the frozen lake surface.

● Besides Isle Royale, the park harbors more than 450 smaller islands
● The island's rocky backbone was formed by a huge, long-lasting lava flow
● Native Americans started mining the island's copper at least 4000 years ago

Isle Royale

Agate Fossil Beds
■ National Monument, Nebraska

* ☀ Miocene-era fossil remains in northwestern Nebraska
* ☀ 20-million-year-old bison, rhinos, camels, and bear dogs
* ☀ Possibly a waterhole where ancient mammals gathered

So, I'm not much to look at now, but 20 million years ago, during the Miocene era, I was crawling with creatures. Not dinosaurs—it was way too late for those supersized lizards —but weird and wonderful mammals that no longer exist.

Take *Dinohyus*, a colossal piglike beast as big as a modern bison. Or *Palaeocastor* beavers that lived in corkscrew-shaped burrows rather than underwater lodges. And how about *Menoceras* rhinos, a mini camel called a *Stenomylus*, and ferocious, meat-eating *Amphicyon* "bear dogs" that preyed on all the others. Native Americans discovered the old bones long before rancher James Cook came across my fossil beds in the 1880s. Because many of the bones were close together, paleontologists believe the ancient animals died around a waterhole during droughts.

* ● Miocene fossils and Native American artifacts are displayed at the visitor center
* ● Current critters include coyotes, deer, snapping turtles, and nighthawks
* ● Agate also preserves mixed-grass prairie and wetlands along the Niobrara River

Agate Fossil Beds

Effigy Mounds
■ National Monument, Iowa

☀ 200 earthen mounds on the west bank of the Mississippi River
☀ Created by the Eastern Woodland people (600–1250 C.E.)
☀ Decorated with images of birds and bears

Built between 850 and 1500 years ago, I am one of the greatest artistic achievements of the Native American Woodland Culture that flourished along the Mississippi River. People lived in towns nearly as big as those in Europe, traded a wide variety of products along routes that spanned North America, and constructed earthen mounds shaped like animals—in my case, bears.

I have the Marching Bear Group around my southern end and the Great Bear Mound up north, measuring 137 feet (42 meters) from nose to tail. These effigies (images) were probably inspired by the mound builders' spiritual beliefs and reflect the life that existed around them in the ancient sky, water, and forest. Some historians believe the mounds may also have marked boundaries between rival tribes.

● Located in the Driftless Area, a part of the Midwest that was never glaciated
● Effigy Mounds appears on the Iowa "America the Beautiful" quarter (2017)
● Situated along the Mississippi Flyway, more than 290 bird species visit the park

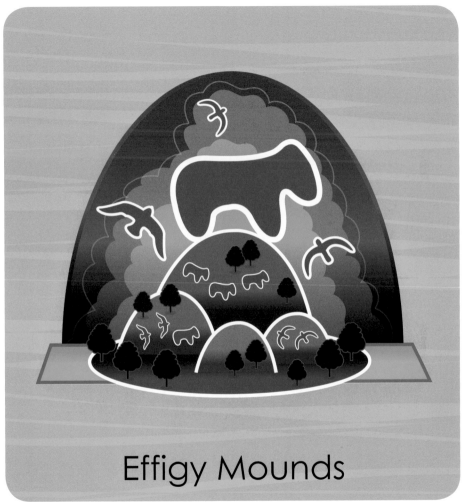

Effigy Mounds

Voyageurs
■ National Park, Minnesota

✳ Watery wooded wilderness in northern Minnesota
✳ Named for 18th-century French trappers and traders
✳ Includes four major lakes along the U.S.-Canada border

Ever wondered why so many Midwest places (including mine) have French names—like Detroit, Des Moines, Terre Haute, and St. Louis? It's because French trappers and traders roamed the region before it became part of the United States. Those *voyageurs* ("travelers") covered vast distances in birchbark canoes made by the Ojibwe people.

Around 40 percent of me is covered in water, including the four large lakes I share with Canada. No prizes for guessing that the best way to get to know me is paddling my remote waterways on canoe camping trips. From black bears and beavers to moose and gray wolves, there are plenty of animals you could meet along the way. And after dark, my sky is magical, filled with the same stars the old-time *voyageurs* once slept beneath.

● Motorists can drive "ice roads" across two of the park's frozen lakes in winter
● Native Americans once harvested and ate wild rice that grew naturally here
● The park's ancient greenstone is some of Earth's oldest rock (2.8 billion years old)

Voyageurs

Ice Age
■ National Scenic Trail, Wisconsin

✳ One of just 11 national scenic trails in the United States
✳ Follows the outer edge of Wisconsin's Ice Age glaciation
✳ Stretches from Lake Michigan to the Mississippi River Valley

You wanna hang out with me, you had better be prepared to walk some. That's because I'm a 1200-mile (1900-kilometer) trail that links debris hills called moraines and drumlins with boulders known as erratics, and other geological features created by glaciation.

I came about during the series of Ice Ages that covered much of North America until around 10,000 years ago. Back then, a lot of superheavy snow and ice got moved around as glaciers grew and retreated. Dips in Earth's surface were created in the process and eventually filled with water that became the many lakes you find along my route. Glaciers also carried lots of rocks, dirt, and debris across the landscape. When the ice finally melted, my erratics, moraines, and drumlins were left behind.

● The last major period of the Ice Age is called the Wisconsin glaciation
● Thirty of Wisconsin's 72 counties feature sections of the trail
● Some pre–Ice Age rocky outcrops along the trail are 1.8 billion years old

Ice Age

Mount Rushmore
■ National Memorial, South Dakota

✳ The faces of four presidents carved in a Black Hills mountain
✳ Sculpted by Idaho-born artist Gutzon Borglum over 14 years
✳ The four heads are each as high as a six-story building

Gutzon Borglum made me what I am today. Literally. He sculpted images of four presidents—Washington, Jefferson, Teddy Roosevelt, and Lincoln—into my stone face. He chose me over all the other mountains in the Black Hills because of my big, wide granite wall and the fact that I face southeast for maximum morning sunshine.

In case you didn't notice, I'm not exactly finished. When he started chiseling away at me in 1927, good old Gutzon envisioned four head-to-waist figures. But the project was costly. It took the artist and his team 14 years to complete what you see today—the faces and Washington's collar—before the money ran out. But it didn't matter, because people still flocked to see me. I became an American icon and am the focus of millions of selfies each year.

● Mount Rushmore's granite erodes around 1 in (2.5 cm) every 10,000 years
● A team of more than 400 men helped Borglum create the presidential faces
● Jackhammers and dynamite were the main sculpting tools

Mount Rushmore

Gateway Arch
■ National Park, Missouri

* ☀ Stainless steel arch with elevators to a lofty viewing area
* ☀ Tallest man-made monument in the western hemisphere
* ☀ Forty city blocks were cleared to make space for it

At first glance, I'm a giant stainless steel arch that towers 630 feet (190 meters) above the waterfront in downtown St. Louis. But dig a little deeper, and you'll discover that I'm also a symbol of America's westward expansion from the Mississippi River to the Pacific Ocean. Since I was finished in 1965, I've come to represent other important ideas.

The Old Courthouse at my feet is where African-American slave Dred Scott and his wife, Harriet, famously sued for their freedom in the 1840s and 1850s. Belowground, my museum highlights all of those who shaped the American West, from Native Americans to explorers Lewis and Clark. And from my waterfront wharf, you can board riverboats *Tom Sawyer* and *Becky Thatcher*, named in honor of author Mark Twain, who was born just upriver from me. Full steam ahead!

* ● Until 2018, the park was called the Jefferson National Expansion Memorial
* ● Finnish-American architect Eero Saarinen designed the arch
* ● The Scotts' case went all the way to the U.S. Supreme Court before they lost

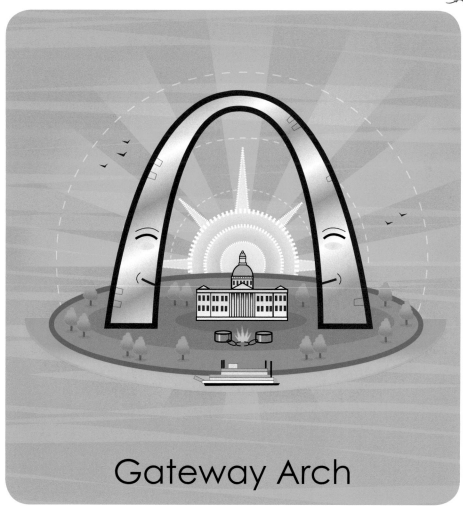

Gateway Arch

Theodore Roosevelt
■ National Park, North Dakota

* Preserves Theodore Roosevelt's log cabin and ranch site
* Roosevelt served as U.S. president from 1901 to 1909
* He lived in the Dakota Badlands between 1883 and 1887

I'm named for Teddy Roosevelt, who came to my Dakota badlands in 1883 to hunt bison. He returned the following year to start a cattle ranch and stayed through some of the toughest winters I've ever known. There's not much left of his Elkhorn Ranch other than stone ruins, but the Maltese Cross Cabin where he stayed that first year still sits near the park entrance.

Theodore Roosevelt

● "Badlands" are areas of desertlike rock formations carved by wind and water
● Bison, prairie dogs, and wild horses are the park's big-three animal species
● The park hosts the Dakota Nights Astronomy Festival in August or September

Indiana Dunes
■ National Park, Indiana

�֍ 15 miles (24 km) of beach and dunes along Lake Michigan
✳ Started to form around 6000 years ago, after the last Ice Age
✳ This shape-shifter moves around 4 ft (1.2 m) inland each year

Indiana Dunes

Sand dunes at the Great Lakes? You bet! At the bottom edge of Lake Michigan, my dunes rise behind a long beach where visitors can swim, fish, or even scuba dive. Trees and other plants grow on my sandy "hills," and in the dips are bogs, grasslands, and swampy areas like the Great Marsh, home to beavers, butterflies, and many different kinds of birds.

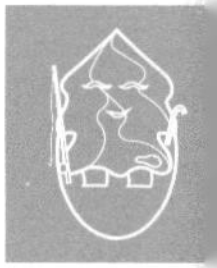

- The sand here makes a "singing" sound when walked on
- There are more varieties of orchids here than in all of Hawaii
- The dunes once supplied sand to a glass fruit-jar factory

Chapter 4
The Rockies

When they first crossed the Rockies, 19th-century explorers and pioneers were astounded by the natural wonders they saw—and the sights are no less impressive today. You see, there's more to this region than its hulking mountains. There are geysers, glaciers, and deep gorges, stories of huge animal herds, and mysterious ancient cities built into canyons and cliffs. Yellowstone is here, a vast wilderness that spans parts of Wyoming, Montana, and Idaho with wildlife, woods, and bubbling waters. Other treasures include Zion and Bryce Canyon in Utah, Glacier in Montana, and Mesa Verde in Colorado.

Glacier

Yellowstone

Rocky Mountain

Mesa Verde

Arches

Bryce Canyon

Zion

Glacier
■ National Park, Montana

✳ Vast mountain landscape carved by glaciers
✳ Blackfoot is the largest of the park's 26 surviving glaciers
✳ Going-to-the-Sun Road crosses the park from east to west

People call Montana Big Sky Country, so you can call me Big Sky Park. Not because of my wide-open spaces and endless panoramas (although they're awesome), but for the way the clouds, peaks, forests, and glaciers reflect in my many lakes. It's like having two skies instead of one.

My east side is on the dry, rain-shadow side of the Rockies, which means I've got a sunny disposition. Even the twisty highway that runs up and over me is called Going-to-the-Sun Road. People driving the route might meet some of my friends: grizzly bears and mountain goats, bald eagles, and bighorn sheep. Stop and say "hello" to my Canadian neighbor, Waterton Lakes National Park in Alberta province. Together, we're an international peace park dedicated to the long friendship between our countries.

● The park has more than 700 lakes—only 131 of them have names
● Only 26 of 80 glaciers have survived the last 150 years of climate change
● Lake McDonald, the park's largest lake, has red, green, and blue rocks

Glacier

Yellowstone
■ National Park, Wyoming, Montana, & Idaho

❋ Founded in 1872, this is the world's first national park
❋ A giant super-volcano lies deep beneath the park
❋ Bison, bears, elk, and wolves are among its inhabitants

I may be an old-timer, but I'm fizzing with activity—just take a gander at my geysers. Old Faithful erupts 20 times a day, blasting gallons of scalding mist 106 feet (32 meters) into the air. My 500 geysers (half the world's total!), mud pots, hot springs, and fumaroles are all powered by a super-volcano beneath my surface. The last time that hothead erupted, it left a 1500-square-mile (3900-square-kilometer) crater that's still there . . . and that was 640,000 years ago!

All that heat draws animals like a magnet! My critter count includes 67 mammal species and 330 bird species. Come spring, North America's largest wild herd of bison ambles in to munch on young grass. Those big boys are hard to miss, but only the lucky few get to glimpse my three cat species (cougar, lynx, and bobcat) or the wolverines and weasels.

● About 96% of the park lies in Wyoming, with 3% in Montana and 1% in Idaho
● In terms of area, it's larger than Rhode Island and Delaware combined
● Its turquoise-hued Grand Prismatic Spring is bigger than a football field

Yellowstone

Rocky Mountain
■ National Park, Colorado

☀ Home to mountains that formed 35 to 65 million years ago
☀ Features 60 peaks over 12,000 ft (3600 m) in elevation
☀ Sees more than 270 species of birds through the year

Sure, the Rockies stretch from Montana to New Mexico, but only my small Colorado home carries national park status. Seeing as I represent everything the range is famous for—lofty peaks, ancient glaciers, alpine lakes, and thick evergreen forests—I truly deserve the honor.

I'm the result of a geological process called plate tectonics. Don't try this at home, but imagine writing the names of the continents on plates and sliding them around the kitchen floor. When one plate slips under another, that second plate is raised higher off the ground. That's how my mountains formed—giant tectonic plates in motion, running into one another and lifting up Earth's surface. My animal counts are elevated, too: in summer, some 3000 elk graze large meadows called "parks" on my eastern edge.

● Ecosystems range from montane meadows and forests to Arctic-like tundra
● The park's Trail Ridge Road is the highest continuous highway in the country
● Longs Peak is the park's highest point (14,259 ft/4346 m)

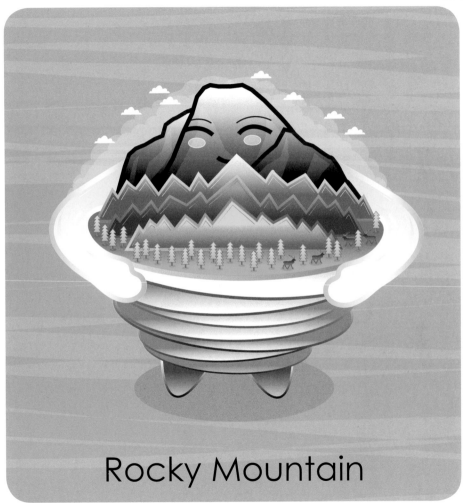

Rocky Mountain

Mesa Verde
■ National Park, Colorado

✳ Home to more than 4500 archeological sites
✳ Some 600 cliff dwellings dating from the 1190s to the 1270s
✳ Has been deserted since around 1300

Spanish explorers called me *mesa verde* ("green table") because I'm a flat tree-covered mountain that rises high above the desert. While my natural design is undeniably awesome, I'm world famous for man-made architecture—namely some of the region's most spectacular cliff dwellings.

Constructed with sandstone, mud bricks, wooden beams, and plaster, the structures were built in difficult locations so that enemies couldn't reach them. One of them, Cliff Palace, housed around 100 people in 150 rooms on several levels connected by wooden ladders. The Ancestral Puebloans who built the dwellings suddenly left one day, and no one knows why. Researchers think it could have been drought, famine, or tribal disputes. It remains a history mystery that may never be solved.

● Many cliff dwellings have kivas—usually round rooms used for ceremonies
● The Ancestral Puebloans are also known for their baskets and pottery
● Elk are common in the park, and there are bears and mountain lions, too

Mesa Verde

Arches
■ National Park, Utah

☀ More than 2000 red-rock arches in southeastern Utah
☀ Includes the much photographed Delicate Arch
☀ Cactus species include prickly pear and whipple's fishhook

Oh, I'm popular now, but that hasn't always been the case. When I first opened in 1929, just 500 people came to see my legendary stone arches. With only rough dirt roads and primitive cars, it was hard for folks to reach me back then.

No, it wasn't until the invention of social media that folks really noticed my ruddy good looks, showed up on my doorstep, and asked me to be in their selfies. Nowadays, one-and-a-half-million people a year drive a crazy zigzag road through my wilderness, which is spangled with more than 2000 arches and other awesome red-rock formations. Formed by millions of years of wind and water erosion, my fabled Landscape Arch and its siblings are Mother Nature's artwork, geological sculptures as grand and impressive as anything created by humankind.

● Landscape Arch is a record-breaking 290 ft (88 m) wide
● Formation names include Dark Angel, Park Avenue, and Sheep Rock
● It's so hot in the desert, most of the animals come out only at night

Arches

Bryce Canyon
■ National Park, Utah

※ A series of red-rock amphitheaters rather than a true canyon
※ Features hundreds of tall, thin stone pillars called hoodoos
※ Named for 1875 Scottish pioneer Ebenezer Bryce

I wouldn't be the park I am today without my old friend Coyote. A sacred being to the Paiute people, Coyote is a trickster, but he can be a savior, too. Take the time he challenged the ancient Legend People who refused to share food and water with other living things. He turned them into tall, thin stone pillars that the Paiute called *anga-ku-wass-a-wits* ("red-painted faces"). Nowadays, these red-rock pillars are called hoodoos, and I've got more of them than any other place on the planet.

No disrespecting Coyote, but modern scientists say my hoodoos formed over millions of years by water seeping into my stone cliffs and then freezing on cold nights. The ice expands and creates cracks that grow big enough to make tall, skinny rock formations that break away from the cliffs.

● Part of the Grand Staircase region stretching south to Zion and the Grand Canyon
● High altitude, clear skies, and remote location make Bryce ideal for stargazing
● One of the last homes of the endangered Utah prairie dog

Bryce Canyon

Zion

■ National Park, Utah

☀ Spectacular canyon country with rivers and waterfalls
☀ More than 90 miles (145 km) of hiking trails of varying difficulty
☀ Named for the Hebrew word for "refuge"

If you like hiking, feel free to stomp all over me! I've got some of the most awesome trails in the entire National Park System. The Narrows trail that passes through Virgin River Gorge is knee-deep in water in places. Perched high above the river, Angels Landing really does look like a place where angels might hang out. If you don't have wings, the only way to reach the clifftop lookout is walking up a series of steep switchbacks and then across a narrow rock ridge with a 1490-foot (455-meter) drop on either side. Reaching Kolob Arch—the world's second-longest natural stone arch—is best done as a two-day hike.

I've got easy hikes, too: an Archeology Trail leading to the ruins of an ancient Native American village and a trail to the gorgeous Emerald Pools and their misty waterfalls.

● Four ecosystems: desert, riparian (riverside), pinyon-juniper, and conifer forest
● The park has more than 1000 native species of plants
● Park predators include coyotes, ringtail cats, and gray foxes

Zion

Chapter 5
The Southwest

Let's get one thing straight: the Southwest is not all boring desert! The region's national parks prove that places like Arizona, New Mexico, and West Texas feature an incredible variety of landscapes and cultural treasures. Sure, the Grand Canyon is the region's undisputed superstar, but there are plenty of parks with awesome adventures. You can toboggan down the snowlike dunes of White Sands, take an underground hike at Carlsbad Caverns, or canoe down the Rio Grande in Big Bend. Saguaro safeguards the world's biggest cacti, while Petrified Forest preserves some of its oldest trees.

Grand Canyon

Canyon de Chelly

Saguaro

Petrified Forest

White Sands

Big Bend

Carlsbad Caverns

Grand Canyon
National Park, Arizona

✳ A long, steep-sided valley carved out by the Colorado River
✳ It's taken 5 to 6 million years to sculpt the canyon the way it is
✳ Stretches 18 miles (29 km) across and is 1 mile (1.6 km) deep

At 277 miles (446 kilometers) long, I'm surely one of the world's most colossal gaps. I was born 5 to 6 million years ago, when the Colorado River started flowing across land that was once the bottom of the ocean. Hiking from my highest point to my lowest point is like traveling from Canada to Mexico when it comes to the difference in plants and animals.

The first Native Americans settled along my rim some 10,000 years ago. Today, the Navajo, the Hopi, the Hualapai, and the Havasupai all live in and around me. I have a colorful personality: deep purple during summer thunderstorms, snow white after a winter flurry, and a blush of golden red at sunrise and sunset. Lots of people hike through me, and it's a blast to see visitors raft my raging whitewater rapids.

● The canyon is bigger than the state of Rhode Island
● It snows at the top in winter; the canyon floor sees summer highs of 120°F (49°C)
● The canyon's oldest rocks, Elves Chasm pluton, are almost 2 million years old

Grand Canyon

Canyon de Chelly
National Monument, Arizona

☀ One of North America's longest continuously inhabited places
☀ Has cliff dwellings constructed by the Anasazi (700–1300 C.E.)
☀ Native animals include jackrabbits and chipmunks

Sure, several national parks have cliff dwellings, but how many parks are still inhabited by Native Americans? The Navajo graze horses and sheep and cultivate crops in the shadow of my massive red-rock walls. They also help park rangers preserve my fragile oasis-like ecosystem and cultural treasures such as Mummy Cave, where their ancestors were buried in yucca-fiber wraps.

Canyon de Chelly

● Archeologists say that people have been living here for around 5000 years
● Around 80 Navajo families live in log-and-mud-brick homes called hogans
● The National Park Service and the Navajo Nation manage the park jointly

Saguaro
National Park, Arizona

- Occupies two settings in the Sonoran Desert
- Named for the nation's tallest cactus species, the saguaro
- Nearly 2 million saguaro cactus plants live inside the park

Saguaro

Say my name: *Sah-wah-row*. Some say I'm prickly, but I'm easy to explore on foot, by horse, or car. Thanks to my cacti, I'm a beloved symbol of the Wild West. I've been painted, photographed, and sculpted countless times, and I've even starred in films. I have real cowboys, too, the wranglers who lead horseback rides through my saguaro forests.

- Saguaro can reach 60 ft (18 m) in height and live as long as 200 years
- More than 400 movies and TV shows have been shot in and around the park
- Some saguaro cacti have microchips so they can be identified if stolen

Petrified Forest
National Park, Arizona

※ Stone "logs" that were living trees 200 million years ago
※ A chemical reaction changed the wood into stone
※ Features the Black, Blue, Jasper, Crystal, and Rainbow forests

I may look, feel, and act like stone nowadays, but once upon a time, I was a lush forest of living trees. That was more than 200 million years ago during the Late Triassic period—the so-called Dawn of Dinosaurs when those giant creatures first appeared. I was part of a tropical ecosystem with trees spread along a river inhabited by giant prehistoric crocodiles. Pterosaurs perched in my branches, and snakelike lepidosaurs slithered through the undergrowth.

The petrified logs you see today were knocked down by floods or volcanic eruptions and buried beneath volcanic ash. Silica in that ash helped crystallize the wood into quartz rock flecked with iron, carbon, manganese, and other minerals that caused my rainbow streaks.

● There are almost a dozen species, including conifers, tree ferns, and gingkoes
● At 7–8 on the Mohs hardness scale, petrified wood is nearly as hard as diamond
● The air here is so pure, it has a rating of Class I—the highest level possible

Petrified Forest

White Sands
National Park, New Mexico

* Snow-white gypsum sand dunes in southern New Mexico
* Gypsum dunes are always cool to lie or walk on
* One of the nation's newest national parks (established 2019)

Yes, I am unbelievably white. No, I am not made of snow! So, what causes my ghostly pallor? I'm made from gypsum, a mineral that gets dissolved by snow and water, then washes down from the surrounding mountains to create me, the world's largest gypsum dune field. You may have never heard of gypsum, but I bet you use it every day. It's an ingredient in shampoo and toothpaste, sidewalk cement, the chalk you write with on blackboards, and plaster casts for healing broken bones.

Hearty little critters such as the Apache pocket mouse, darkling beetle, and an earless lizard somehow manage to live among my rolling dunes. But I think the strangest creatures are the humans who scream and shout as they zip down my dunes on snow saucers and toboggans.

- The park has the largest concentration of Age of Mammals footprints in the U.S.
- Species of white insects, lizards, and moths have adapted to the environment
- Strong winds can bury the park road in sand in a matter of hours

White Sands

Big Bend
National Park, Texas

⚹ Desert, mountain, and river landscape in Texas
⚹ The Rio Grande flows along the park's southern edge
⚹ Eighth-largest U.S. national park outside of Alaska

Yep, I've got a big bend, a colossal curve in the Rio Grande between West Texas and Mexico. My wilderness protects everything from cactus and sagebrush desert to wetlands, grasslands, and forested mountains roamed by black bears and mountain lions. I was carved by water flowing across and eroding a rocky plateau over millions of years.

Santa Elena, my deepest canyon, has 1500-foot (460-meter) walls that shoot almost straight up from the river. That huge bulge in my midsection is no potbelly. It's the Chisos Basin, a mountain range formed by volcanoes that erupted 35 to 44 million years ago. I had a lot of dinosaur pals back in the day. Pterosaurs with 36-foot (11-meter) wingspans, giant prehistoric crocodiles, and three-horned *Chasmosaurus*. You'll meet some of them in my outdoor fossil museum.

● Big Bend has the longest and most diverse fossil history of any national park
● Comanche warriors once traveled back and forth to Mexico on Big Bend trails
● Terlingua and Lajitas ghost towns are just outside the park

Big Bend

Carlsbad Caverns
National Park, New Mexico

* 120 caverns hidden beneath the New Mexico desert
* Has underground rock formations with very strange names
* Lechuguilla Cave stretches at least 145 miles (233 km)

Beneath the rugged desert hills of New Mexico, I'm part of an ancient coral reef now honeycombed with numerous limestone caverns. Some of them, such as Lechuguilla Cave, are among the largest and longest anywhere on Earth.

My rooms are decorated with speleothems—fantastical rock formations created by water creeping down from the surface and slowly dissolving the limestone into something that resembles melted candle wax. Their forms have funny names such as soda straws, lily pads, and popcorn. Some of my rock formations—the Witch's Fingers and Devil's Armchair—were named by a teenage cowboy who got to know me during the Wild West days. Nobody knows how big I am. Spelunkers (cave explorers) are still finding new underground rooms to this day.

● The caverns are inhabited by many thousands of Brazilian free-tailed bats
● In 1932, an elevator replaced guano buckets to take visitors into the caverns
● At 510 ft (155 m), a pit called Kansas Twister could hold a 51-story building

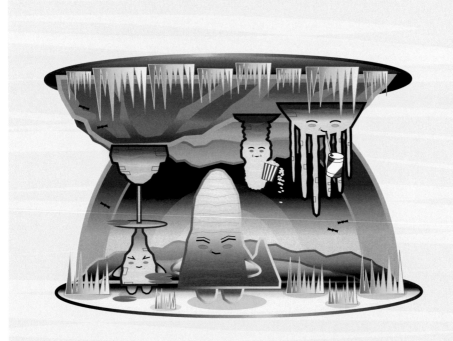

Carlsbad Caverns

Chapter 6
The West Coast

It's not all about the surf, sand, and sun. The West Coast has awesome mountains, valleys, and deserts, too. Kings Canyon, Yosemite, and Sequoia are all high up in the Sierra Nevada, while the Mojave Desert is home to two of the largest and most beloved desert parks: Death Valley and Joshua Tree. Head to Olympic National Park in Washington State to see America's most famous rain forest or Crater Lake in Oregon for one of the world's deepest, most beautiful lakes. But none draw as many visitors as Golden Gate National Recreation Area in San Francisco, the National Park System's most popular destination of all.

Olympic

Crater Lake

Yosemite

Sequoia &
Kings Canyon

Death Valley

Joshua Tree

Redwoods

Channel Islands

Golden Gate

Olympic
National Park, Washington

✳ Tall mountains and temperate rain forests on the Pacific coast
✳ Named after Mount Olympus of Greek mythology
✳ Wilderness home of eagles, salmon, and mountain lions

The Amazon isn't the only place with rain forests. I have them, too, but there's a difference. That huge green space in South America is filled with a tropical jungle. Mine, on the other hand, is cool. The major thing we have in common is lots of wet (*rain* forest, see?). We also have similar, yet strikingly different, animals. Instead of colorful parrots, I've got speedy peregrine falcons. Rather than fearsome jaguars, my resident big cat is the mountain lion. And salmon swim in my rivers and streams, not piranhas!

I occupy most of the Olympic Peninsula, with the Pacific on one side and the Puget Sound (an inland sea) on the other. My highest peak is Olympus. We were named by an 18th-century English sea captain who thought we looked as heavenly as the home of the ancient Greek gods.

● The park's bright-yellow banana slugs can grow up to 10 in (25 cm)
● Hoh Rain Forest averages more than 12 ft (3.6 m) of rain each year
● Blue Glacier in the Olympic Mountains is big enough to hold 20 trillion ice cubes

Olympic

Crater Lake
National Park, Oregon

☀ Deepest lake in the United States (1943 ft/592 m)
☀ Created 7700 years ago when a giant volcano erupted
☀ Has hydrothermal (volcanic) vents on its lake bed

Folks say I'm deep. I like to think they're talking about my brainy intellect, but they're referring to my extreme water depth. You see, I'm one of the world's top ten deepest lakes. You could sink the nation's tallest building in me, and its lofty spire wouldn't even break the surface.

I haven't always been so splashy. I was once a volcano called Mount Mazama. Some 7700 years ago, I blew my top! The eruption created a huge crater that eventually filled with rainwater and snowmelt to create the gorgeous deep-blue lake you see today. Two geological oddballs break my glasslike surface: a jagged outcrop called Phantom Ship and Wizard Island, which you can visit on a boat tour. The island bears no relation to Hogwarts, but is a volcanic cinder cone shaped like a wizard's hat.

● The water is so pure that light reaches 131 ft (40 m) below the surface
● Moss grows deeper here than anywhere else on Earth (400 ft/122 m)
● The lake sees 43 ft (13 m) of snow a year—1.4 in (3.5 cm) a day, on average

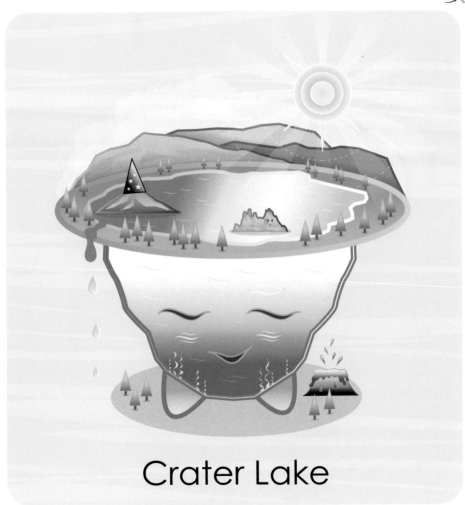

Crater Lake

Yosemite
National Park, California

* A granite landscape carved by glaciers
* Formed between 2 to 3 million and 10,000 years ago
* Has an impressive 800 miles (1300 km) of trails to explore

Yosemite Mountaineering School sells a T-shirt that says, "Go Climb a Rock." No prizes for guessing why! I have cliffs that zoom more than 3000 feet (915 meters) straight up from my valley floor. I have granite domes shaped by long-ago glaciers. And I have jagged peaks in the High Sierra that wear snowy coats the whole year through. I'm known for waterfalls, too—some of the tallest and most beautiful cascades anywhere on Earth, don't you know?

My landscape is a reminder that I got off to a rocky start. Abraham Lincoln tried to save me (along with the Union) during the Civil War, but I was still under threat from ranchers, miners, and lumber companies. It took 22 years of urging by Scottish-American naturalist John Muir before I finally became a national park in 1890.

● Anywhere from 300 to 500 black bears roam the park at any one time
● This is one of the few places in the U.S. where you can see a rainbow at night
● Yosemite Falls plunges an impressive 2425 ft (740 m)

Yosemite

Sequoia & Kings Canyon

National Parks, California

* Two parks that protect 40 ancient giant sequoia groves
* The oldest sequoias first sprouted 3400 years ago
* Mount Whitney: the country's highest point outside of Alaska

Like most twins, we have much in common: big valleys, snowcapped mountains, massive trees. The largest trees on Earth, as it happens: *Sequoiadendron giganteum* (giant sequoia, to you). They can grow to a whopping 275 feet (83 meters) tall. General Sherman, the biggest, weighs more than 6000 tons—equal to around 30 blue whales.

Beyond the redwoods are the giant canyons and peaks of the High Sierra. With its towering granite walls, Kings Canyon is Yosemite's baby cousin. Kern Canyon in the backcountry is known for whitewater rafting. And crowning the Sierra crest of Sequoia National Park is 14,494-foot-tall (4418 meters) Mount Whitney.

- The biggest sequoias weigh around 58 billion times more than their tiny seeds
- President Coolidge declared General Grant Tree the "Nation's Christmas Tree" (1926)
- Bats, tree frogs, salamanders, and flying squirrels inhabit sequoias

Sequoia & Kings Canyon

Death Valley
National Park, California & Nevada

☀ Hottest, lowest, and driest national park in the United States
☀ Largest national park outside of Alaska
☀ The park's Eureka Dunes are more than 680 ft (207 m) high

I'm hot. I mean, really hot. And I'm not talking about my rugged good looks—my record-breaking temperatures get close to 130°F (54°C) almost every summer. Why do I get so heated? Well, my home is the Mojave Desert, which is pretty warm to begin with. But I'm also the lowest point in North America and surrounded by superhigh mountains, a geological phenomenon that makes me like a giant oven.

I'm not nearly as nasty as my sinister name suggests. All sorts can survive and even thrive in this heat: bobcats and bighorn sheep, roadrunners and rattlesnakes. Native Americans weathered my moods for hundreds of years, and prospectors weren't deterred by my fiery nature either. A group of careless covered-wagon pioneers gave me my name after they got lost taking a shortcut, the fools.

● Total area: 3,422,024 acres (1,384,844 ha.)
● World's hottest air temperature: 134°F (57°C) on July 10, 1913, at Furnace Creek
● North America's lowest point: 282 ft (86 m) below sea level at Badwater Basin

Death Valley

Joshua Tree

■ National Park, California

☀ Mojave wilderness with giant boulders and awesome plants
☀ An official "dark sky park" because of its cloudless nights
☀ Famous for UFO sightings and musical superstars

It's said that pioneers named my namesake plant for Joshua in the Bible, its raised "arms" having guided them across the Mojave Desert. Musicians have sought inspiration in me, rock climbers have clambered over my boulders, and some folks think UFOs land here. Deep down, I'm just a good old desert park where visitors can camp beneath a star-filled sky.

Joshua Tree

● The park's namesake tree is one of more than 750 resident plant species
● Big and spikey, Joshua trees aren't real trees but giant succulents
● Native Americans used Joshua trees to make sandals, baskets, and red dye

Redwoods

■ National & State Parks, California

✴ Stretches 40 miles (64 km) along the Northern California coast
✴ Safeguards five of the world's six tallest trees
✴ Hyperion Tree is the world's tallest living thing (380 ft/116 m tall)

Redwoods

A merger of three state parks (plus a little extra), I'm a great protector of woody giants. So protective that the location of my tallest tree, Hyperion, is a closely guarded secret. Some of my trees are at least 2000 years old—mere saplings when the Roman Empire was flourishing. Their genetic roots stretch all the way back to Jurassic days when dinosaurs walked the earth.

● Many of the park's tallest trees, including Hyperion, are named for Greek gods
● Scenes from *The Lost World: Jurassic Park* were filmed here, in Fern Canyon
● The big trees "hold hands" with one another by intertwining their roots

Channel Islands

National Park, California

* Shelters five of eight Channel Islands off the California coast
* Animal and plant species that exist nowhere else on Earth
* Native Americans started living here around 12,900 years ago

Who says time travel isn't possible? Because visiting me is like cranking back the clock to California of long ago. To the Wild West sheep and cattle ranchers who once owned my islands. To the mariners who planted Spanish royal flags here. To the Chumash people who harvested my seaweed, shellfish, and other bounties. And even to my pygmy mammoth inhabitants of 20,000 years ago.

You see, since I became a national park in 1980, I've gone back to nature, to be the way I was before the first humans arrived. The mammoths are long gone, but I've got plenty of other animal friends both on land and in the ocean around me. Some of them exist nowhere else on Earth—like the island fox, island night lizard, island spotted skunk, and Santa Cruz Island gopher snake.

- Painted Cave on Santa Cruz Island is one of the world's largest sea caves
- The northern fur seal colony on San Miguel Island has around 10,000 creatures
- The bright-orange Garibaldi fish inhabits the kelp forest around the islands

Channel Islands

Golden Gate
National Recreation Area, California

☀ Most popular National Park System destination
☀ Draws around 15 million visitors each year
☀ Shelters 19 different ecosystems from beaches to wetlands

Everyone thinks I'm named for that bridge or how the sunset colors the cliffs at the entrance to San Francisco Bay. Truth be told, one of the first Americans to visit me figured I was just as impressive as the Golden Horn, the watery passage that separates Europe and Asia. The name stuck, and my reputation grew.

I was upset when they built that giant steel span across my mouth (who likes braces?). But over time, the bridge grew on me—literally. I don't like to brag (or maybe I do), but I probably have more variety than any other park: wild ocean beaches and redwood groves; wetlands and ranch lands; a maritime museum and marine mammal rescue center; Civil War forts, Alcatraz prison, and even a statue of Yoda. Yeah, I'm more than just a pretty bridge.

● Golden Gate Bridge connects the park's Marin County and Bay areas
● Alcatraz Island was a federal prison from 1934 to 1963
● The movie studio that makes Star Wars films is now based here, at the Presidio

Golden Gate

Chapter 7
Alaska & Hawaii

The Pacific Ocean island chain and the frozen north were racking up national parks long before they even became American states. In 1916, Hawaiian Volcanoes on the Big Island and Haleakala on Maui were among the first members of the National Park System. Alaska's Glacier Bay, Katmai, and Denali peak—the highest mountain in North America—were soon welcomed into the family. While the Hawaiian parks feature colossal volcanoes and their unique tropical ecosystems, the Alaska parks shelter a wide variety of landscapes and wildlife, from glaciers, fjords, and Arctic tundra to grizzly bears, whales, and caribou.

Denali

Wrangell-St. Elias

Glacier Bay

Kenai Fjords

Katmai

Haleakala

Hawaii Volcanoes

Denali

National Park & Preserve, Alaska

* Home to the highest mountain in North America
* Features more than 12,200 lakes and ponds
* Home to just one kind of amphibian, the tiny wood frog

Someone has to be the tallest kid in the (national park) class, and my namesake peak is exactly that. At 20,310 feet (6190 meters) from head to toe, Denali is the tallest mountain in North America. Lack of oxygen on my upper slopes, dangerous crevasses in my glaciers, and below-zero temperatures even in the middle of summer make me a very difficult climb, but people still try. Only around half them make it all the way to the top.

My name means "the high one" or "the tall one" in the language of the Koyukon Athabaskan people who have lived for centuries in the tundra and forest around the base of my peak. Due to the huge amount of snow that falls on me each winter, rangers have to patrol with sled dogs. At any one time, I have around 30 canine friends for company.

- At 9500 square miles (24,600 sq km), Denali is bigger than the state of New Hampshire
- The park and peak were originally called Mount McKinley after the 25th president
- Around 600 climbers reach the top of Denali each year

Denali

Wrangell-St. Elias
■ National Park & Preserve, Alaska

☀ Largest U.S. national park (six times bigger than Yellowstone)
☀ Has North America's greatest glacier count
☀ Home to one of the world's biggest active volcanoes

Imagine Alaska before humans came across the Bering Strait land bridge, and you'll picture me—a vast wilderness that hasn't changed in millennia. Nearly everything about me is superhuge, including many of the highest peaks and largest glaciers in North America, as well as untamed whitewater rivers and remote waterfalls that no one has ever named.

My outdoor toybox includes Alaska's longest and deepest caves, one of the world's biggest active volcanoes, and an enormous bay filled with icebergs that break off my tidewater glaciers. I have wildlife aplenty, from sea lions and sea otters along the coast to grizzly bears and caribou that rove my woodland and tundra. Together with Glacier Bay and two Canadian parks, I form one of the world's largest protected wilderness areas.

● Skilled bush pilots can land planes on beaches, glaciers, and mountainsides
● The park's Kennecott Copper Mine is a national historic landmark
● Malaspina, a massive piedmont glacier, is larger than the state of Rhode Island

Wrangell-St. Elias

Glacier Bay

■ National Park & Preserve, Alaska

☀ Glaciers currently cover 27% of the park
☀ Only around 50 of the park's 1045 glaciers have names
☀ The longest, Grand Pacific Glacier, stretches 34 miles (55 km)

Around 90 percent of the people who show up at my front door arrive by cruise ship. Massive tidewater glaciers—which tumble down to the ocean from some of the highest peaks in North America—make it virtually impossible to visit me any other way. I've got seven of those frozen giants.

Two of my tidewater glaciers tower 250 feet (75 meters) above the bay. The cloudy blue color of their ice reminds me of cotton candy. That amazing hue is caused by thousands of years of being crushed and condensed by the weight of the glacier. The ice becomes so dense it absorbs every color except blue. Glaciers have a wild side. I like to think of them as frozen giants emitting a deafening roar as they hurl giant blocks of ice into the bay . . . you could say I have a very active imagination!

● As many as 329 fish species have been recorded in the park
● Leatherback sea turtles are the park's only known reptile
● Harbor seals give birth to their pups on icebergs that have calved off the glaciers

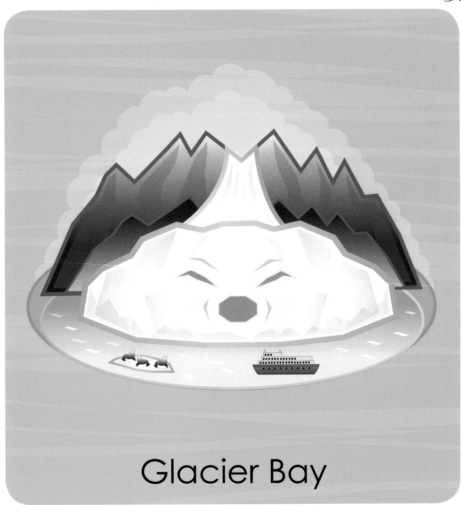

Glacier Bay

Kenai Fjords
■ National Park, Alaska

✳ Marine wildlife sanctuary along the Gulf of Alaska coast
✳ Long, deep bays and colossal glaciers
✳ Inhabitants include dolphins, whales, sea lions, and sea otters

When John Muir made the quote in the Introduction to this book, he was referring to people and their need to reconnect with nature. In my case, he could just as well have been talking about wild animals.

I was created in 1980 to give wildlife a forever place to meet, mingle, and raise their young. A dozen different types of marine mammals seek peace and quiet in my fjords—long, narrow, deep channels filled with seawater. We're talking everything from sea lions and dolphins to six different whale species, including black-and-white orcas and huge fin whales. People have to visit me by boat or floatplane, and practically the only way for them to stay overnight is camping. It means I never get overcrowded (or even busy) and my animal guests can feel safe.

● Around 51% of the park is covered by glaciers and ice fields
● The park coastline stretches for more than 545 miles (880 km)
● Kenai nurtures one of the world's northernmost temperate rain forests

118

Kenai Fjords

Katmai

■ National Park & Preserve, Alaska

- ✸ Located near the top of Alaska's remote Aleutian Peninsula
- ✸ Famous for large, active volcanoes and vast lava fields
- ✸ World's largest concentration of brown bears (around 2200)

In the fall, Fat Bear Week is when people send photos of my bears taken before and after the feeding season. You should see their roly-poly transformation! To gain weight for hibernation, brown bears gulp dozens of salmon each day. They wouldn't get through an Alaska winter without it. Some of them—Scare D Bear, Beadnose, and 747 (jumbo-jet size)—are good friends of mine.

Katmai

- ● The Valley of Ten Thousand Smokes was created by a 1912 volcanic eruption
- ● NASA astronauts used Katmai's lava fields to simulate walking on the moon
- ● Spawning salmon provide abundant food for the park's many bears

Haleakala

National Park, Hawaii

- ❋ Volcano towering 10,023 ft (3055 m) above the island of Maui
- ❋ Active, and last erupted 400 to 600 years ago
- ❋ Only place in the world where the silversword plant grows

Haleakala

The ancient Hawaiians called me Haleakala, or "House of the Sun," because it seems you can almost touch the solar orb from my summit. Every morning, I welcome hundreds of visitors who drive up my twisty road to watch the sunrise over the Pacific Ocean. It can be really cold at the break of day, and people wrap up warm until the sun pokes its face above the horizon.

- ● Waterfalls tumble down rain forest ravines in the park's Kipahulu District
- ● The park is home to 250 to 350 nene geese, Hawaii's official state bird
- ● People can hike and even camp overnight in the huge volcanic crater

Hawaii Volcanoes
■ National Park, Hawaii

☀ Site of two of the world's most famous volcanoes
☀ A shield volcano, Mauna Loa is Hawaii's biggest volcano
☀ Kilauea has been erupting for around 40 years

I'm known for my bubbly personality—bubbling with lava, that is! Kilauea has been spewing molten material since 1983. The funny thing about Kilauea is that he's not your typical conical-shaped volcano, but just a big hole in the ground surrounded by lava-leaking cracks. Mauna Loa is much bigger but not nearly as dangerous. Measured from seafloor base to summit, she rises 30,000 feet (9140 meters)—that's a greater height than Mount Everest!

Away from the lava fields, I'm a plant paradise. Rich volcanic soil nurtures big rain forest trees, delicate ferns, and gorgeous tropical flowers. My shoreline is too rough to surf. But you see the same stretch of Pacific that ancient Polynesians sailed across when they first arrived in Hawaii from the South Pacific around 1600 years ago.

● According to Hawaiian legend, Kilauea is home to the volcano goddess Pele
● So much of Mauna Loa is underwater that it doesn't rank as the world's tallest peak
● The park's dark, desolate Ka'u Desert mixes lava rocks, pumice, and volcanic ash

Hawaii Volcanoes

Index

Glossary

Appalachian Trail: Long-distance hiking trail stretching more than 2190 miles (3525 kilometers) from Georgia to Maine along the crest of the Appalachian Mountains range.

Archeologist: A scientist who studies human history and culture by digging up and analyzing artifacts, tombs, buildings, and other items.

Archipelago: A chain of ocean, sea, lake, or river islands that are close to one another in the same geographical area.

Barrier island: A sandy island running parallel to a shore that protects the coast from storms and helps create wetland areas in which plants and animals thrive.

Biodiversity: The variety of plant and animal species in a specific region, area, habitat, or environment.

Biosphere: The part of the earth where life can exist or a specific ecosystem that supports life.

Canyon: A deep and often narrow valley with steep sides, created by rivers, glaciers, earthquakes, and other geological forces.

Colony: A village, town, or larger living space created by people from a specific nation who continue ties with their mother country.

Continental divide: A geographical boundary, almost always in mountains, that marks the separation of rivers and streams that flow into different oceans.

Dark Sky Park: An area considered ideal for viewing the stars because of its clear air and lack of light pollution from cities or other sources.

Ecosystem: A place of living and nonliving things that interact with one another and the surrounding environment.

Erosion: The act of wind, waves, rain, ice, and other natural forces wearing away rock or soil.

Fjord: A long, deep valley partially filled with ocean water and typically formed over thousands of years by glaciers.

Fumarole: A crack or similar opening in the earth's surface that releases steam or gas created by volcanic activity.

Geology: The study of the earth's physical structure, as well as the rocks and other materials that create that structure.

Geyser: A natural spring that shoots a column of steam and hot water high into the air.

Glacier: A large body of dense snow and ice that slowly moves down a mountain or valley.

Gorge: An especially deep and narrow canyon, often with a river or stream running through it.

Ice field: A huge expanse of snow, ice, and glaciers over a very large area.

Immigrant: A person who leaves their home country or region and moves permanently to a foreign land.

Lagoon: A shallow coastal body of water separated from an ocean or a sea by a barrier island, coral reef, peninsula, or other geographical barrier.

Lava field: A rocky landscape caused by molten lava flowing from a volcano and then cooling off.

Glossary

Mangrove swamp: A partially submerged coastal wetland with dense vegetation that helps protect the shore and nurture local marine life.

Maritime: Anything that has to do with the ocean or sea, from ships and fishing to navigation and underwater nature preserves.

Mortar: A paste used for binding building blocks such as stones and bricks, which hardens as it dries.

Naturalist: A scientist, nature guide, or other expert who studies plants, animals, and other aspects of natural history.

Paleontologist: A scientist who studies ancient life forms (such as dinosaurs) by digging up and examining their fossils.

Peninsula: A piece of land nearly surrounded by water that extends into an ocean, sea, lake, or other body of water.

Preserve: An area selected for the protection and preservation of wild plants and animals.

Presidential inauguration: The ceremony in Washington, DC during which a newly elected president is sworn into office.

Reserve: A piece of land that preserves and protects animals, plants, geological features, bodies of water, and other natural features.

Tidewater: The water in a bay, estuary, or other coastal area affected by the ebb and flow (rise and fall) of tides.